R Blackwell

KU-094-651

TRADE UNIONS AND
THE ECONOMY

MACMILLAN NEW STUDIES IN ECONOMICS

Published

Brian Burkitt and David Bowers
TRADE UNIONS AND THE ECONOMY

Keith Cuthbertson
MACROECONOMIC POLICY: THE NEW CAMBRIDGE, KEYNESIAN
AND MONETARIST CONTROVERSIES

M. C. Howard
MODERN THEORIES OF INCOME DISTRIBUTION

Homa Katouzian
IDEOLOGY AND METHOD IN ECONOMICS

In preparation

Sanjaya Lall
TRANSNATIONALS AND THE LESS DEVELOPED COUNTRIES

TRADE UNIONS AND THE ECONOMY

Brian Burkitt
and
David Bowers

© Brian Burkitt and David Bowers 1979

All rights reserved. No part of this publication may be
reproduced or transmitted, in any form or by any means,
without permission.

First published 1979 by
THE MACMILLAN PRESS LTD
London and Basingstoke
Associated companies in Delhi Dublin
Hong Kong Johannesburg Lagos Melbourne
New York Singapore and Tokyo

Printed in Great Britain by
LOWE AND BRYDONE PRINTERS LTD
Thetford, Norfolk

British Library Cataloguing in Publication Data

Burkitt, Brian
    Trade unions and the economy. – (Macmillan new
    studies in economics).
    1. Trade unions – Great Britain
    2. Great Britain – Economic conditions – 1945–
    I. Title   II. Bowers, David
    331.880'941   HD6664

    ISBN 0–333–25993–9
    ISBN 0–333–25994–7 Pbk

This book is sold subject to the standard conditions of the Net Book
Agreement.

The paperback edition of this book is sold subject to the condition that it shall not, by
way of trade or otherwise, be lent, resold, hired out, or otherwise circulated without the
publisher's prior consent in any form of binding or cover other than that in which it is
published and without a similar condition including this condition being imposed on the
subsequent purchaser.

For

Brenda and Eve

CONTENTS

ACKNOWLEDGEMENTS

The authors and publishers wish to thank the following, who have kindly given permission for the use of copyright material:

Australian Bureau of Statistics, for a table from *Industry Information Bulletin* (January 1966) and a table from *Official Year Book of Australia*.

Foreign Press Centre – Japan, for figures from *Japan's Year Book of Labour Statistics* (1977).

Gower Press, for a table from *Trade Unions in Europe* (1974), by M. Stewart.

The Minister of Supply and Services, Canada, for statistics from *Canada Year Book* and *Union Growth in Canada* (1970).

National Bureau of Economic Research Inc., for a table from *Trade Union Membership 1897–1962*, by L. Troy.

1
Introduction

This book analyses the economic aspects of trade-union operations in a capitalist society.[1] It assembles the results of previous research into the consequences of union actions and attempts to evaluate current controversies about their impact on the economy. Inevitably the conclusions that we draw are based in part upon subjective opinions and our political philosophy. Trade unions are so important and controversial a phenomenon that it would be impossible to find a neutral observer to write a book of this kind. Moreover, discussion of their effects is complicated by the confusion of two distinct issues: the first, what their actual effects are; and the second, whether these are beneficial or harmful.

We try to accumulate as broad a cross-section of professional research and opinion as the length of the book permits. We are aware, however, that like all writers on union affairs the degree of emphasis we accord to various topics and the manner in which we approach them are conditioned by our political perspective. We cannot eliminate this perspective, nor would we wish to, but feel it is essential that we should state explicity our fundamental value judgements concerning union activity. We hope that readers keep these judgements continually in mind and consult some of the work we quote that embodies a contrasting approach to ours. Although we declare our philosophy in this introduction, we are aware that much of it is controversial, so that throughout the book we have kept in mind the importance of allowing readers to draw their own conclusions from the material we present.

We reject the currently fashionable view that trade unions are 'too powerful' which appears to be held by the mass media, many politicians and a growing section of the public. We believe that unions are less powerful than employers, whose possession of the means of production enables them to command decision-making procedures.

It is true that some groups of workers can exert considerable bargaining power because they perform key tasks and are supported by cohesive organisations, while over a wide spectrum of industry unions have accumulated greater strength over the last forty years. However, employers remain dominant since they control the crucial productive decisions (e.g. on output, employment and investment) subject to only limited legal and union restraints. Individual workmen occupy a weak bargaining position in most circumstances, so that unions introduce an element of democracy into an otherwise autocratic work environment by attempting to curb the power of capital through collective organisation. This point of view is currently in danger of neglect; thus much current discussion of industrial disputes seems to us ill-focused, since strikes should be perceived against the background of unequal power. On such a perspective the common attitude which largely blames workers for stoppages of work becomes an oversimplification, because collective action is essential to check the unilateral exercise of employers' authority. However, collective action, like other sources of bargaining power, can be abused.

Economists have traditionally analysed the operation of labour markets as a special case of the price mechanism,[2] but this method involves a number of problems. Workers own only their labour power which they must sell to maintain themselves and their families, but capitalists own funds that enable them to command man-made means of production and so possess bargaining advantages when negotiating terms of employment with individual workmen. Unequal bargaining power and the resulting market imperfections are normal, rather than isolated, occurrences when labour is unorganised.

Labour's weakness in negotiations, the dominance of those supplying capital and the interrelationship between economic and political power are phenomena which may create a demand for workers' organisations to increase their bargaining power. This demand stimulates the development of trade unions, which attempt to establish negotiating rights over their members' wages and conditions of employment. Unions do not introduce power considerations into labour markets, but prevent competition between workers and harness their numerical strength to produce a 'countervailing power'. When workers act as individuals their ultimate sanction is to change their job, which carries the threat of a period of unemployment. Unions possess a wider range of bargaining weapons, while their resources and negotiating expertise enable them to identify favourable opportunities and present demands with greater skill, aggression and market knowledge.

Phelps Brown (1957b) argued that the formation of unions was a response to industrialisation, which placed individual workers at a bargaining disadvantage while subjecting them to a discipline that was essential for efficient factory production. Moreover, cyclical and technological unemployment posed the threat of financial insecurity. Yet the demand for organisation is not equally insistent in all labour markets; thus unions flourish in printing, but fail to develop in temporary office employment. Union growth rests not only on workers' needs but also on their awareness of need and their ability to organise. The degree of unionisation in any trade depends upon individual workers' perceptions of the balance of advantages and costs, which vary over time as well as with the nature of the job. None the less trade unions are a *natural* consequence of the character of labour markets and not exogenous, unnatural or disturbing.

Because of the rarity of perfect competition[3] in labour markets, power is an integral feature of their operation, made explicit by the development of collective bargaining. Neoclassical theory concentrated upon the establishment of equilibrium under competition on the assumption that the price mechanism was the major method of taking economic decisions, but imperfections create an uneven distribution of power which may be exploited to alter the market mechanism or to affect its results. Moreover, the conditions within which labour's supply and demand interact may be changed by the effective deployment of power. The emphasis upon competition has yielded analytical insights but the operation of bargaining strength requires greater attention from economists than it has yet received. In these confusing circumstances professional students of labour markets tend to divide into two groups, economic theorists and industrial relations experts, each often believing in the irrelevance of the other. Only isolated attempts have been made to integrate theory and practice.[4]

This book aims to contribute towards such integration through an analysis of the major areas of trade-union economic activity. The task is attempted by removing unrealistic neoclassical assumptions, e.g. a perfectly competitive labour market is regarded as exceptional. Market analysis is placed within the context of social relations – which can influence the methods of production; thus the laws and conventions

relating to property ownership affect the control of income opportunities and the distribution of output. Technical change and social
development are interrelated. Changes in productive techniques
modify social conditions, e.g. the building of railways, but production
and distribution can vary between economies in the same state of
technical knowledge when their systems of resource ownership differ
(see Robinson and Eatwell, 1973). Therefore, the social character of
employer–worker relations provides the framework within which
labour markets operate.

SYNOPSIS OF THE SUCCEEDING CHAPTERS

Chapter 2 analyses the imperfections existing in unorganised labour
markets which place workmen at a bargaining disadvantage with
their employers and thereby stimulate trade-union development. We
consider some of the influences that determine the demand for union
services and the changing structure of union organisation, while
fluctuations in the degree of unionisation over time are discussed.

Chapter 3 looks at the scope available for one union to change
wage differentials in its members' favour and traces the extent to
which an association has been discovered between relative wages and
the strength of trade unions across labour markets. It has not proved
difficult to find some association, but its strength varied between
different types of differential, different countries, different industries
and different periods. Consequently the extent to which unions influence the pattern of differentials remains a controversial issue.

Chapter 4 analyses the phenomenon of a cost-push inflation at
national level, either inaugurated or accelerated by union pressure
for higher money wages. This pressure became more effective under
the changed labour-market conditions brought about by the maintenance of full employment between 1940 and 1970.

One of the major aims of the union movement is to secure a
fundamental redistribution of income in favour of workers. Changes
in the share of the national product claimed by labour and property
are described in Chapter 5 and the opportunities available to unions
for increasing the proportion paid to labour are considered.

Trade unions do not restrict themselves to bargaining about their
members' wages but also attempt to achieve more favourable non-
pecuniary conditions of work. The employment contract subjects
workers to factory organisation and discipline, which unions attempt

to modify by entering into manpower management. Chapter 6 defines various possible relationships between capital and labour in terms of the shifting frontier of control between employers' authority and the rights achieved by unions for their members.

All these aspects of union activity possess consequences for society as a whole, so that governments become inextricably involved in labour markets. Chapter 7 considers the relationship between the state and trade unions. Traditionally, U.K. governments supported voluntary collective bargaining and reduced their intervention to a minimum, but such a policy became untenable during the last decade. In particular the strengthening of tendencies towards cost-push inflation stimulated the search for alternative strategies to achieve the simultaneous existence of full employment and stable prices under current labour-market conditions. This led to attempts by the state to restrict union operations and to control the determination of prices and incomes.

Chapter 8 stresses the inadequacy of conventional theories of labour-market operation given the importance of bargaining power and suggests that a more embracing theory of trade-union activity is required.

2

An Economic Analysis
of Trade-Union
Development

INTRODUCTION

Economists usually portray the process of wage determination as an extension of the theory of value in which the role of competition is emphasised with the aid of concepts developed in other branches of economic theory, for instance marginal analysis based on income-maximising assumptions. Labour-market institutions in general, and the development of trade unions in particular, tend to be discussed separately and are conventionally regarded as 'distortions'. Such an approach implies that the existence of unions is abnormal, and that compared with the operation of 'free' market forces they work to the detriment of the economy, even if they prove to be a source of relative advantage to specific groups of workers.

It is unlikely that a perfectly competitive labour market has ever existed; when the economic conditions of the parties concerned are unequal, legal freedom of contract enables the superior in strength to dictate terms. Workers own only their labour power, which they must sell to maintain themselves and their families, but capitalists own funds that enable them to command man-made productive resources, and so possess the bargaining advantage when negotiating wages and working conditions with individual workmen. The formation and growth of trade unions is a response to the inequality of bargaining strength in most unorganised labour markets which stimulates a demand for collective employee organisations to negotiate, and thereby improve, wages and working conditions. The widespread existence of such organisations can hardly be regarded as exceptional 'distortions'.[1]

THE FACTORS PROMOTING INEQUALITY OF BARGAINING POWER
IN UNORGANISED LABOUR MARKETS

There are many causes of employer dominance in unorganised labour markets. Industrialisation created a sizeable class whose only means of livelihood was the sale of its labour power. The necessity for an immediate sale is overwhelming: workers may accumulate savings, but these are usually small in relation to family commitments, so that a failure to sell labour power produces a substantial drop in living standards in a short space of time. An inability to complete negotiations between employers and individual workmen leads to a loss of potential income for each, but this loss will be more severe for the worker, since the employer can often replace the services of one man. Even when this proves impossible, the loss of profit is rarely complete and may be offset by a rearrangement of the remaining workforce.

Wage-earners suffer from the relatively short duration of their contracts; before the Contracts of Employment Act of 1963[2] these could normally be terminated at a week's notice, so that all workers were quickly at the mercy of fluctuations in the demand for labour. By contrast, while the incomes of businessmen and professional staff vary over a long period, they are fairly predictable in the short run. As a result of their limited resources and inability to enter into long-term contracts, most workers suffer from financial insecurity. Consequently unless labour is scarce they tend to accept whatever wages and conditions are offered during individual negotiations. Labour power cannot be stored because every day of unemployment involves a loss of part of the asset. It is more vulnerable than capital, which can be maintained intact for future use even when losing potential current income.

Usually a large number of sellers of a specific type of labour confront a smaller number of buyers, so that a worker has fewer alternatives available if he is dissatisfied with the terms offered. Competition for jobs tends to be greater than competition for workmen, and greater competition produces a disadvantageous negotiating position. The sheer fact of numbers also makes it harder for workers to fix a minimum acceptance wage informally, and then enforce it, than for employers to agree upon a maximum offer.

Most individual workers lack the relevant knowledge for wage bargaining. They are ignorant of their value to a particular employer, and tend to be imperfectly aware of alternative job opportunities.

The employer, on the other hand, controls the flow of revenue from which wages are paid, so that he alone knows the gain obtained from recruiting an additional worker. He also knows the current price of labour in other local firms and, approximately, in other regions. The employer's greater knowledge extends to the art of bargaining; his experience of wage negotiations is usually wider, so that he can often achieve his desired goal by skilful manipulation of the weak position of most potential employees. He is accustomed to issuing orders and obtaining obedience, while his status in society is greater than that of his workers. All these influences contribute to employers' dominant position in wage negotiations. The consequent market imperfections are a normal occurrence in the absence of trade-union organisation.[3]

Employer dominance extends beyond wage negotiations to a control of the productive process and the behaviour of workers participating in it. Employers and workers may be equal parties at law to an employment contract but they are never equal in practice. When industry is privately owned its fundamental dynamic is the earning of profits; the suppliers of capital, or their hired representatives, take all important production decisions, while labour is treated as a marketable commodity and the individual worker's livelihood is at the mercy of economic and technological changes. The employment contract inevitably subordinates workers to a structure of managerial discipline, which is designed to maximise the effort and application they supply in return for wages: the job environment, hours of work and behaviour in the factory are prescribed for them. Workers cannot change these conditions without managerial consent, but employers can initiate change unilaterally by issuing orders that they expect to be obeyed. The employment contract is thus inherently unequal: the ownership of capital becomes an instrument of social control and a legally free sale of labour power involves some surrender of the worker's freedom.

The quantity of capital required to put technological advances into effect has risen substantially since the eighteenth century until the amounts necessary are now far larger than most people can acquire during a lifetime. The scarcity of the ability to supply finance on the scale needed for industrial efficiency enables those who possess it to secure a commanding economic position.

The disparity in the bargaining strength of employers and unorganised workers has been denied by a number of economists. For instance, Hutt (1973) argued that there will be no unequal bargaining advantage if the individual worker is free to withdraw his labour after due notice and can refuse to work at the wage offered. The actions of collective organisations then become restraints of trade. Such a view fails to recognise the importance of differential power in labour markets where few alternatives exist, since employers are unable to find another workforce easily and the workers as a group cannot find other employment. In these circumstances every transaction depends to some degree upon force and inequalities exist between individuals buying and selling labour.

In response to these inequalities workers seek to increase their bargaining power and to protect themselves from managerial control; this search stimulates the formation and growth of trade unions. Unions attempt to establish negotiating rights over their members' wages and conditions of work, so that the labour force becomes involved, through its elected representatives, in the determination of its job environment. Such involvement is impractical outside very small establishments without formal union organisation. Trade unions aim to defend, and hope to improve, their members' standard of living and social status. Successful policies to achieve this have repercussions that extend beyond the immediate bargaining situation, since their overall effect is to limit the power of employers, whose arbitrary authority is replaced by agreed rules. Unions thus seek to limit managerial authority over labour after its hire in addition to improving wages and conditions of work.

THE DEMAND FOR TRADE-UNION SERVICES

The demand by workers for collective organisation to counteract the bargaining strength of those owning capital is not equally insistent under all circumstances; thus workers become more aware of their common interests when employed in large rather than small establishments and in urban rather than rural environments. The growth in demand for union services is influenced by the occurrence of events which inject a consciousness of their unfavourable position into the lives of the unorganised. Trade-union development depends upon workers' awareness of their needs and upon their ability to organise; the emergence of the first stable unions among craftsmen illustrates these points.

Bose (1975) argued that capitalists are 'at the mercy' of their workers as they cannot produce and earn profits without employing labour. Our analysis implies that capitalists and workers can never be equally dependent on each other, while certain conditions must be fulfilled before workers exercise any influence over managerial decisions. First, labour must act as an organised group: a worker depends for his livelihood upon retaining a particular job, but capital relies for its profit not upon the employment of an individual but of a labour force as a whole. Second, labour needs the ability to impose costs upon its employer in the event of a disagreement. Such an ability implies the existence of effective unions capable of remedying the bargaining weakness of individual workers by, for instance, increasing their 'waiting power' and replacing a mass of isolated negotiations by one collective bargain.

Conventional microeconomic theory, reformulated by Holt (1970), analyses labour markets in terms of stocks of unemployed workers and job vacancies, and of a search process for mutually satisfactory bargains; the various flows to and from these stocks generate negative feedbacks which reduce the amplitude of fluctuations and hold the market close to equilibrium. Wage changes are generated by individual offer and acceptance decisions as workers and vacancies flow through the market, and depend upon the aspirations of workers and employers and the rate at which these change with the duration of the search process. These factors undoubtedly influence the process of wage determination, but a theory concentrating upon their operation fails to explain the origin of trade unions in response to the inherent employer dominance of unorganised labour markets.

Once this role of trade unions is appreciated, attention centres upon the phenomenon of bargaining power, which can be defined in a general sense as the ability to get one's own way and in economic terms as the ability of an individual or group to fix or alter the conditions of exchange in its own favour. A crucial aspect of bargaining power is the ability of one party to a negotiation to impose a loss upon the other by refusing to conclude an agreement. The infliction of losses becomes crucial in labour markets, where the employer is unable to recruit an alternative workforce and the workers as a body cannot find alternative employment. Chamberlain (1951) defined bargaining power as the ratio of costs of disagreement to costs of agreement for each party, i.e.

The bargaining power of a trade union =

$$\frac{\text{The cost to the employer of disagreement with the union's terms}}{\text{The cost to the employer of agreement on the union's terms}}$$

$$\text{The bargaining power of the employer} = \frac{\text{The cost to the union of disagreement with the employer's terms}}{\text{The cost to the union of agreement on the employer's terms}}$$

When workers act as individuals their cost-imposing sanction is a change of employment, which involves the risk of a long search for another job. Trade unions can deploy a wider range of sanctions. These include boycotts, blacklists, go slows, working to rule, overtime embargoes and various methods of controlling labour supply, but the most costly is the strike, which involves a temporary but planned withdrawal of labour by a group of employees. Strikes by non-unionists occur occasionally but the development of union organisation is a prerequisite for the imposition of most collective sanctions. Trevithick and Mulvey (1975) argued that unions can articulate wage claims with more skill, aggressiveness and wider market knowledge than individuals, since they enjoy greater resources and specialised bargaining expertise. Thus they are more likely to identify opportune circumstances and to present claims in persuasive terms.

Strikes are the ultimate sanction available to trade unions when attempting to impose their will upon employers, as the chequered careers of those eschewing strike action illustrate (e.g. the National Union of Bank Employees). By withdrawing labour in one body a perfectly elastic supply of workers is created at the desired wage and conditions of work; here employers can recruit whatever numbers they like, but at less desirable wages or conditions the union endeavours to withhold all employment. Strikes are an integral part of capitalist–worker relations, as they enable sellers of labour to exert some control over their purchaser by temporarily refusing to produce. However, the propensity to strike varies between industries. Kerr and Siegal (1954) found a common international pattern in which it was highest in arduous trades with a recognisable 'group-consciousness', though Goodman (1967) demonstrated that strike activity has become more widely distributed across industries.

The relative attractiveness of individual compared with collective sanctions varies with the level of economic activity. For both employers and workers the cost incurred when an individual quits his job is associated with the rate of unemployment: as unemployment increases, quit costs rise for the worker and fall for the employer. To a company these costs comprise the time and money expended in obtaining a replacement, the loss of sales revenue from the output forgone during the duration of the vacancy and the reduced productivity from any short-time working involved when hoarding labour in anticipation of quits. To a worker a quit involves loss of income during the search for a new job, the psychological stress of being without work and the risk of an ultimately lower wage. The search process can be initiated from either side of the labour market as firms seek workers and workers seek jobs, but its relative urgency alters at different phases of the trade cycle. When unemployment is high employers secure their labour force with little search effort and 'success' in wage negotiations is more difficult for individual workers to achieve. When unemployment is low employers intensify recruitment campaigns and their search effort rises, while the average cost of a job change for the worker falls.

Once workers become effectively organised in trade unions they can undertake collective sanctions that interfere with the employers' income more decisively than do individual job quits; the loss of one worker, replaced after a varying time lag, affects production and sales revenue less than group action. The cost which union weapons impose upon the employer is related to economic conditions. Both parties always suffer losses, but the employer is hurt most, and labour's bargaining power is highest, when demand and prices are large. Workers suffer a greater loss of potential wages when striking during a boom but they are likely to possess more savings to compensate, while the risk of losing their jobs to 'blacklegs' is less.

At full employment workers can impose heavier costs upon employers in the event of disagreement, whether acting as individuals or in organised groups. The costs inflicted by individual and union sanctions decline absolutely when unemployment rises, but those of individual sanctions fall most. In Figure 2.1 the absolute power wielded by unions falls with an increase in unemployment but the relative differential attached to union membership rises. Trade unions obtain wage increases in conditions of full employment but so do unorganised workers, because employers bid against each other for scarce labour; the union wage differential drops, as individual quit threats become more costly relative to the impact of strike action. However, collective bargaining possesses an increasing advantage over individual negotiation as a worker strategy when unemployment increases. Most workers are reluctant to threaten quits when alternative jobs are difficult to obtain, nor do such threats seriously inconvenience employers as vacancies can be filled from those out of work. Union bargaining weapons hurt employers less when profits are low, but they may still modify company policy by interrupting its flow of revenue.

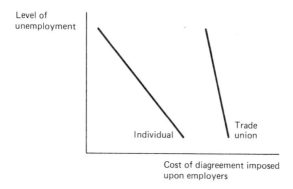

Figure 2.1

Therefore, economic conditions affect the value of trade-union membership. The demand for union services from potential recruits depends upon the benefits relative to the costs of membership. During recruitment campaigns promises of wage gains are made which must be redeemed to ensure loyalty. A wage increase stimulates prospective members to join the relevant union, from gratitude, guilt or expectation of future gains. Joining a union involves the payment of subscriptions, which may be a marginal item in many budgets so that higher wages allow more workers to meet the cost of union membership.

Trade-union wage pressure becomes one method of obtaining recruits; Dunlop (1944) discussed this strategy in terms of a membership function,[4] such as *MF* in Figure 2.2. The higher is the money-wage impact of a union, the greater is the proportion of potential members who join it. The slope of the membership function reflects a marginal relationship, i.e. the increment in the number of workers affiliated to a union which is associated with each increment in the wage rate. If the union seeks to maximise its membership, it sets the wage rate at the position where the labour-demand schedule intersects the membership function (e.g. at OW_1 in Figure 2.2).

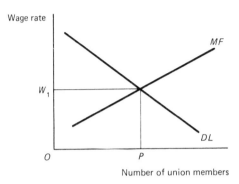

Figure 2.2

The position of membership functions changes with the level of economic activity. When they shift downward the wage increase necessary to achieve a given degree of unionisation declines; union organisation extends to groups where its (unchanged) wage impact was previously too low to attract adherents. This process occurs during full employment, when the cost of union membership stemming from the risk of long strikes to achieve particular goals is low. Similarly, government policy facilitating unionism or discouraging disputes by the provision of arbitration procedures pushes membership functions downward. In a depression the risks of job loss through strike-breaking or victimisation and the possibility of long strikes to enforce claims rise, as does the cost of unemployment, so that the functions move upward.

Trade unions secure economies of scale in negotiation for their members, but they cannot alleviate all the bargaining weaknesses of individual workers, because employers continue to control the revenue from which wages are paid and the ownership of property remains unequally distributed. Therefore, the scope for union action is constrained by the socio-economic environment within which collective bargaining occurs.

THE TREND TOWARDS CENTRALISATION

In order to reap the benefits of negotiating economies of scale, trade-union organisation tends to become increasingly centralised. The first stable unions were formed among craftsmen, concerned to defend their relative position against the mass of unskilled labour. They were local in orientation, aimed at maintaining wage differentials to their members' advantage and indulged in restrictive practices to limit entry to their organisation and the relevant labour market. Responding to technical developments in production and transport, which assembled large numbers of workers in sizeable firms and cities with a similar way of life, mass unions grew alongside, and sometimes replaced, the craft organisations. As unions spread among unskilled workers, they became fewer, aimed at the largest possible membership and tended to recruit on an industrial rather than a craft basis. The growth of unions created an administrative bureaucracy, whose existence in turn reinforced the trend to centralisation. Collective bargaining was established in some U.K. industries by the beginning of the twentieth century at a district level (e.g. coal-mining), but many union fights for recognition had still to be won. The existence of national negotiating machinery was rare at this time.

This stage of labour-market organisation led to a further transition, marked by increasing concentration of industry and a greater government involvement in economic affairs. Unions organised on an industry-wide basis operate increasingly on the national plane, where a greater number of decisions are taken. Strikes become more widespread in character, and key disputes are often waged at strategic points in the public sector. Frequently wage claims focus on a single absolute or percentage figure, so that the wage structure tends to diminish in range. The nature of collective bargaining changes as it becomes more extensive; trade unions no longer fear that wage gains create unemployment among their members, because employers cannot replace them with cheaper labour. In practice the union movement now represents all workers, whether organised or not. Individual unions cannot act easily in isolation since the success of their policies depends partly on the support they receive from other unions. The miners' strikes of 1972 and 1974 were assisted by the refusal of lorry drivers and power workers to cross picket lines, while the defeat of the postmen in 1971 became more likely with the telephonists' refusal to co-operate. Each union operates within a socio-economic environment in which its every action creates potential precedents for others to follow.

National economic variables become significant criteria during collective bargaining. Thus after a period of inflation the behaviour of the general price level enters trade-union strategy, though the impact of wage changes upon the rate of inflation and the balance of payments cannot be resolved by individual union action. Political initiatives involving the whole movement are required; the talks between the government, the T.U.C. and the C.B.I. concerning general economic policy over the last decade illustrate the process by which unions have developed from isolated local bargaining units into one body capable of influencing, and being influenced by, the pattern of economic development. The growth of the economic impact of union activities is linked in Europe to the advance of working-class political parties, since collective-bargaining success is intimately related to wider political changes such as universal suffrage and welfare legislation.

Therefore, the overall trend of trade-union development has been towards centralisation, as unions endeavour to influence a wider range of variables that determine their members' living standards. This general tendency has coexisted since 1940 with the growth of workshop negotiations, whose importance was enhanced by a period of continuous full employment.

THE DEGREE OF UNIONISATION

Table 2.1 provides details of the degree of unionisation in the United Kingdom during the twentieth century (for details on the rest of the world, see the appendix to this chapter). Between 1911 and 1921 union membership more than doubled, partly due to unions' success in increasing money wages during a period of labour shortage. Their status improved as a result of war-time collaboration with the government, while the automatic application of arbitration awards illustrated their functions and powers to potential recruits. Membership functions fell, as full employment removed fears of blacklisting and replacement by the unemployed during a strike. Consequently the degree of unionisation rose from 17.1 per cent in 1911 to 34.3 per cent in 1921. Thereafter it suffered a continuous decline until 1933, except for a slight upward movement in 1924. The decline began with the loss of over two million members in the 1921 slump, when unions

Table 2.1   The degree of unionisation in the United Kingdom
(1901–74)

Year	Male	Female	Total	Year	Male	Female	Total
1901	16.2	3.2	12.4	1948	55.6	24.2	45.1
1911	21.7	6.2	17.1	1949	55.1	23.8	44.5
1921	41.2	17.6	34.3	1950	54.6	23.4	44.0
1923	40.5	16.4	32.9	1951	55.6	24.6	44.9
1924	41.1	15.9	33.1	1952	55.8	24.9	45.0
1925	40.1	16.0	32.4	1953	55.1	23.9	44.3
1926	37.4	15.4	30.4	1954	54.7	23.8	43.9
1927	34.8	14.9	28.4	1955	55.0	23.6	44.2
1928	33.5	14.6	27.5	1956	54.5	24.4	43.9
1929	33.3	14.3	27.2	1957	54.7	24.2	44.1
1930	32.6	13.7	26.5	1958	53.6	23.7	43.1
1931	30.5	13.2	25.0	1959	53.0	23.4	42.6
1932	29.0	13.0	23.9	1960	53.3	23.9	42.8
1933	28.5	12.7	23.5	1961	52.8	24.0	42.5
1934	29.8	12.7	24.4	1962	52.0	24.2	42.1
1935	31.3	13.0	25.0	1963	51.9	24.5	42.0
1936	33.6	13.4	27.2	1964	52.2	24.9	42.3
1937	36.2	14.4	29.3	1965	52.3	25.2	42.4
1938	37.0	14.5	29.8	1966	52.1	25.2	42.2
1939	40.0	15.0	31.6	1967	51.6	25.6	42.0
1940	44.6	15.2	33.9	1968	52.8	26.8	43.1
1941	48.5	17.5	36.3	1969	54.3	28.3	44.5
1942	54.3	20.2	39.3	1970	58.3	31.6	48.3
1943	57.5	22.8	43.1	1971	58.6	32.1	48.6
1944	59.0	23.0	44.2	1972	59.9	33.0	49.1
1945	53.3	21.9	41.5	1973	60.2	33.0	49.2
1946	54.4	22.9	43.5	1974	60.5	34.2	50.1
1947	54.9	23.9	44.4				

Sources: *Historical Abstract of British Labour Statistics, 1886–1968*
(London, H.M.S.O., 1971) tables 109, 196.

proved unable to maintain the post-war level of money wages.
Increased unemployment caused many without jobs to leave their
unions while promoting greater caution in those still at work, and

unemployment remained high until 1939. Membership failed to increase despite rising employment between 1926 and 1929, largely owing to the loss of morale and financial reserves after the General Strike. The changing location of industry intensified problems of recruitment because the growing sectors were located mainly in the Midlands and the South-east, where union penetration was relatively low. At its nadir in 1933 the degree of unionisation stood at 23.5 per cent, but an increase in the following year initiated an upward movement that continued until 1939 in response first to the greater economic activity and then to rearmament.

The Second World War led to a dramatic rise in unionisation from 29.8 per cent in 1938 to 44.2 per cent in 1944, with membership rising from six and a quarter to nearly eight million. Union support for the war effort and their leaders' participation in the machinery of government enhanced their prestige; indeed union co-operation was essential to the conduct of a totally planned war. The scarcity of labour, which lowered the cost inflicted by employers' bargaining sanctions, and union representation on trade boards to determine pay in poorly organised trades led to a downward movement of the membership function, as workers could reap the benefits of unionism at little cost in terms of employer retaliation.

After a fall in 1945 unionisation increased during post-war demobilisation to a peak of 45.1 per cent in 1948. Thereafter it fluctuated only slightly, with a mild downward trend from 45.0 per cent in 1952 to 42.0 in 1967. Bain (1966) argued that this decline was primarily due to the changing composition of the labour force, with strongly unionised industries tending to contract while poorly organised trades expanded; in particular the trend towards non-manual employment militated against the maintenance of union density. From 1967 a strong resurgence of membership reversed the decline in unionisation which increased each year until in 1974 it reached the 50 per cent level for the first time in the history of U.K. trade unionism. The union movement's recent success in attracting previously unorganised workers is related to higher rates of inflation. Bain and Elsheikh (1976) claimed that price rises exert a positive influence upon union growth because workers organise to defend their real living standards against the threat posed by higher prices. Success in this objective stimulates additional recruitment via the membership function. The size of unionisation increases failed to accelerate with price inflation in the early 1970s because increased unemployment and the 1971 Industrial Relations Act[5] raised membership functions by lowering the perceived benefits relative to the perceived costs of unionism. Price and Bain (1976) concluded that economic factors, particularly the level of unemployment and the rate of price inflation, exerted a dominant influence on the growth of unionisation in the last decade, though the impact of legislation also altered the position of membership functions.

CONCLUSION

The operation of unorganised labour markets provides workers with an incentive to develop their bargaining power. The demand for union services arises from an awareness among non-unionised workers of the need to counter employers' dominance. Unions provide economies of scale in negotiating wages and conditions of work for their members, and where they can exert sufficient power they become countervailing institutions to the structure of managerial control over the labour force. However, the relative attraction of individual and group initiatives by workers varies with economic conditions, and the position and slope of membership functions can be used to illustrate changes in the demand for union services. In an attempt to exert their maximum potential bargaining strength trade unions have developed an increasingly centralised structure. Fluctuations in the degree of unionisation in the United Kingdom are positively related to the level of economic activity and the rate of price inflation, though exogenous influences such as two world wars, the General Strike and legislative control of union activities affect this association. In the rest of this book we try to assess the impact of trade-union activities upon certain crucial features of the operation of labour markets in the United Kingdom. This assessment is placed within the context of union development as discussed in this chapter.

APPENDIX: THE DEGREE OF UNIONISATION IN THE REST OF THE WORLD

United States

Year	Degree of unioni- sation	Year	Degree of unioni- sation	Year	Degree of unioni- sation	Year	Degree of unioni- sation	Year	Degree of unioni- sation
1900	3.0	1935	6.8	1943	20.5	1951	23.8	1959	22.3
1910	5.8	1936	7.4	1944	22.2	1952	24.5	1960	23.6
1920	11.8	1937	10.3	1945	22.4	1953	25.7	1961	21.1
1930	6.3	1938	10.7	1946	22.1	1954	24.3	1962	20.7
1931	6.2	1939	11.5	1947	23.2	1955	24.4	1964	22.2
1932	5.8	1940	15.5	1948	23.3	1956	24.3	1965	22.4
1933	5.4	1941	15.0	1949	22.5	1957	24.5	1968	23.0
1934	6.6	1942	17.4	1950	22.0	1958	22.8	1970	22.6
								1972	21.8

Notes: (i) Total trade-union membership is expressed as a percentage of the total civilian labour force; (ii) For the years before 1930 the number of union members includes Canadian members of unions with headquarters in the United States and some other members outside the continental United States.

Sources: (i) 1897–1962 – L. Troy, *Trade Union Membership 1897–1962*, National Bureau of Economic Research, Occasional Paper, no. 92, 1965; (ii) 1964–72 – *Statistical Abstract of the U.S. Bureau of the Census* (U.S. Department of Commerce, published annually).

Australia

Year	Degree of unionisa- tion	Year	Degree of unionisa- tion	Year	Degree of unionisa- tion	Year	Degree of unionisa- tion	Year	Degree of unionisa- tion
1954	61	1963	57	1966	53	1969	50	1972	53
1961	57	1964	56	1967	52	1970	50	1973	54
1962	57	1965	56	1968	51	1971	52		

Note: Unionisation is expressed as a percentage of total wage- and salary-earners.

Sources: (i) *Official Year Book of Australian Bureau of Statistics* (published annually); (ii) *Industry Information Bulletin*, vol. 21, no. 1, Australian Department of Labour and Industry, January 1966.

Canada

Year	Degree of unionisa-tion	Year	Degree of unionisa-tion	Year	Degree of unionisa-tion	Year	Degree of unionisa-tion	Year	Degree of unionisa-tion
1921	9.4	1932	6.7	1943	14.6	1955	23.6	1966	24.5
1922	8.2	1933	6.7	1944	15.9	1956	24.5	1967	26.1
1923	8.1	1934	6.5	1945	15.7	1957	24.3	1968	25.4
1924	7.5	1935	6.4	1946	17.1	1958	24.7	1969	25.4
1925	7.6	1936	7.2	1947	18.4	1959	24.0	1970	25.9
1926	7.5	1937	8.5	1948	19:4	1960	23.5	1971	25.6
1927	7.7	1938	8.3	1949	19.3	1961	22.6	1972	26.6
1928	7.8	1939	7.7	1951	19.7	1962	22.2	1973	28.0
1929	8.0	1940	7.9	1952	21.4	1963	22.3	1974	28.1
1930	7.9	1941	10.3	1953	23.4	1964	22.3	1975	28.6
1931	7.5	1942	12.7	1954	24.2	1965	23.2		

Note: Unionisation is expressed as a percentage of the total civilian labour force.

Sources: (i) 1921–67 – *Union Growth in Canada*, Canadian Department of Labour, Economics and Research Branch, 1970; (ii) 1968–75 – *Canada Year Book* (published annually).

Japan

Year	Degree of unioni-sation	Year	Degree of unioni-sation	Year	Degree of unioni-sation	Year	Degree of unioni-sation
1956	15.1	1959	16.3	1962	19.4	1965	21.2
1957	15.5	1960	17.0	1963	20.1	1966	21.3
1958	15.9	1961	18.3	1964	20.8		

Source: Figures derived from Japan's *Year Book of Labour Statistics* (published annually).

Europe

Year	Degree of unionisation in:							
	Belgium	West Germany	France	Italy	Luxem-burg	Nether-lands	Ireland	Denmark
1958	60	38	23	57	60	43	39	70
1969	67	37	22	57	55	41	48	70
1970	67	37	22	57	55	41	48	70
1971	67	37	22	57	55	41	48	70
1972	66	37	20	57	50	42	52	—

Sources: (i) 1958–71 – M. Stewart, *Trade Unions in Europe* (London: Gower Press, 1974) figure 1, p. 4; (ii) 1972 – E. Jacobs, *European Trade Unions* (London: Croom Helm, 1973) p. 39; (iii) 1972 Ireland statistics – M. Stewart, *Trade Unions in Europe*, table 9.4, p. 120.

3

Trade Unions and Wage Differentials

INTRODUCTION

The economic objective of trade unions is to defend, and hope to improve, their members' real living standards. In this chapter we consider the extent to which the structure of wage differentials relates to union power. We concentrate upon the relative wage impact of unions, which can be defined as the degree to which they raise the wages of those for whom they bargain above what would have been paid in their absence. Since the latter cannot be measured directly, most research tries to compare the level and movement of unionised wages with those paid to non-union or poorly organised workers who are comparable in other respects.[1] Before assessing this research we must discuss the theory of the potential union impact upon wage differentials.

A THEORY OF THE TRADE-UNION IMPACT ON WAGE DIFFERENTIALS

According to the conventional competitive model,[2] equilibrium wage differentials reflect the conditions under which labour is supplied and demanded, so that there is no incentive for workers to transfer employment. When supply or demand in any sector alters the wage structure changes; in response workers transfer to the relatively more lucrative jobs until supply and demand are again equalised throughout the market. However, imperfections in both labour and product markets may constitute an additional source of changes in wage differentials.

The analysis of Chapter 2 suggested that employers normally possess bargaining advantages when negotiating with individual workmen, so that market imperfections produce wages below those that would prevail in a competitive market. Firms that employ a significant proportion of a particular grade of labour cannot obtain an unlimited supply at the existing wage because greater hiring costs are incurred. Additional workers of equal efficiency to the present labour force can be attracted only by increased wages or fringe benefits, while employing workers of lower efficiency or a greater use of overtime leads to higher costs per unit.

Figure 3.1 illustrates the consequences. Because the increased payments needed to obtain extra men must usually be generalised to the existing workforce, the marginal cost of hiring labour (*MC*) rises more rapidly than the supply price of the marginal worker (indicated by the *SS* schedule). Under these conditions, known as *monopsony*, profits are maximised where the additional revenue from extra employment equals the additional costs, i.e. where *DD* interests *MC* in Figure 3.1. Therefore, *OA* workers will be employed at wage *AB* although their marginal revenue productivity[3] is *AC*. The equilibrium wage lies below the marginal revenue productivity, and the marginal cost, of labour.

Trade unions attempt to alter this situation by making uniform wage demands at a higher level. If the employer offers a wage below the union claim, the supply of labour can be temporarily reduced to zero by strike action. Providing that the workforce supports such a policy the union creates a perfectly elastic supply at its wage claim. The monopsonist can no longer reduce wages by cutting employment, while a union may raise wages without causing redundancy. In terms of Figure 3.1 *OA* workers are employed at a wage between *AB*

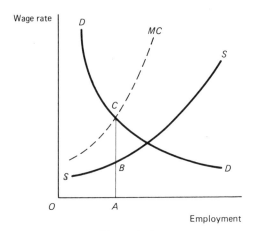

Figure 3.1

and AC, the exact location of which depends upon trade-union bargaining strength; the greater is union power, the closer to AC will be the wage.

When a monopsonist can pay a higher wage to additional workers without increasing the pay of his existing workforce, the marginal cost of labour becomes equal to the wage of the marginal worker. Each employee has a different supply price and is paid only his transfer earnings by the monopsonist, who appropriates the economic rent otherwise received by the intra-marginal workers. Trade unions try to eliminate the profits arising from discrimination by imposing standard wage rates for all individuals.

Since the analysis of Robinson (1933) the possible existence of monopsonistic labour markets has been widely recognised. However, the significance attached to them has been lessened by insistence on the rarity of pure monopsony, i.e. it is difficult to discover many markets with only one buyer of a specific type of labour. The discussion of Chapter 2 implied that employers usually possess bargaining advantages over unorganised workers, which give them partial but not complete monopsony power.[4] In these circumstances unions can raise wages to the level of the marginal revenue productivity of labour without restricting employment opportunities and thus change the wage structure by removing, partially or wholly, the imperfections of specific labour markets due to inequality of bargaining strength. If this occurs, the pattern of differentials alters in accord with the varying degree of union power across markets.

Many economists, for example Rees (1962), argue that once monopsonistic elements are countered union effects on relative wages are limited by the elasticity of demand for their members' services; this determines the cost of a wage increase in terms of lost employment opportunities. Phelps Brown (1966) believed that trade unions redistribute income among workers according to the elasticity of demand they face, with those who gain most having the lowest elasticity and those who lose the highest. Similarly, Hicks (1932) argued that unions possessed the greatest scope to raise wages in those industries which were sheltered from foreign competition.

However, other factors also help to determine the success of a union's impact on wage differentials. The shape of supply and demand schedules is related to social conditions which unions seek to change.[5] Even within a given institutional environment market forces may not yield a determinate equilibrium wage structure. In the short run, when equipment is in fixed supply, the marginal product of labour is indeterminate at full-capacity operation because of the impracticality of varying either the form or the quantity of capital available. This gives rise to a discontinuous demand curve for labour, which is becoming more frequent with the use of increasingly durable and intricate machinery. In these circumstances strong trade unions may push their members' wages up the vertical section of the short-run demand schedule, thus exerting an impact on the wage structure.

In the long run the form and amount of capital used by a firm can be altered, so that greater scope exists for reducing the employment of labour after union-induced wage increases. However, this effect may be offset by changes in the demand for the product; such changes are usually more important over a long period than increasing opportunities of substitution. When demand changes employers and unions often possess conflicting wage objectives, so that unions must exercise power to achieve their aims by imposing costs of disagreement upon employers.

Trade-union bargaining power is one important determinant of short- and long-run changes in the structure of wage differentials. The greater the costs that unions can impose upon employers who refuse to accept their claims, the greater is their strength. We hypothesise that, at any time,

$$W_i = F(M_i, P_i)$$

where W_i is the average relative wage in sector i, M_i represents the market variables acting on sector i and P_i represents trade-union bargaining power in sector i.

A stable wage structure corresponds to a given long-run configuration of market and power phenomena; greater bargaining strength for a particular union leads to a relative wage advantage for its members at a given set of market data. A change in supply or demand and the policies of employers can prevent unions from achieving their objectives, so that relative wages conform both to differential market movements and to differential bargaining power. It is generally agreed that unions may affect the speed of wage adjustment towards equilibrium, but there is little agreement as to whether they create a permanent advantage in their members' favour.

PROBLEMS OF MEASURING THE RELATIVE WAGE IMPACT OF TRADE UNIONS

Before attempting to assess the empirical evidence, the problems of measurement must be considered. Union-induced wage gains may be of two kinds: they could achieve a 'once-for-all' effect upon differentials; or they could obtain a series of upward displacements. Such effects can be measured by cross-section analysis, which compares union wages at one time with non-union wages, or by time-series analysis, comparing movements over time.

Both methods encounter problems. One concerns the difficulty of measuring 'wages' and 'power'. The conventional view of wages is of a rate of return to labour which is flexible to supply and demand movements. Thus hourly or weekly earnings might appear to be the most appropriate measure, since they approximate to what the worker regards as his pay and the employer as his cost. On the other hand, wage rates are closer to the subject of collective negotiations. The use of an index to measure union power presents even greater difficulties, because power is a multi-dimensional concept resting upon political, social and attitudinal, as well as economic, factors.

Estimates of the union impact on relative wages frequently rely on multiple regression analysis, which involves the usual problems of discovering the direction of any casual relationship and of multicollinearity between variables. Measurement of union effects encounters additional difficulties. Lewis (1963) considered that the major cause of error lay in deficiencies of measurement and in errors of adjustment when compensating for non-union influences. The union impact upon relative wages should be calculated for workers of a given quality at given relative conditions of employment, but detailed information on labour quality and non-pecuniary aspects of unemployment is unavailable on a regular basis, though unions may influence both. If a particular group's wages are forced above the competitive level, employers may compensate by raising hiring standards. The relative quality of the workforce improves and the union wage effect is lower than quantified. Conversely failure to adjust for conditions of employment tends to produce an underestimation of union influence, because part of union activity seeks to improve such conditions. These biases of estimate work in opposite directions and the overall effect in any instance is uncertain.

It is impossible to assess accurately what would have occurred in the absense of trade unions. This problem is particularly severe in the United Kingdom, where long-established union influence prevents close comparisons of conditions before and after union development. It is difficult to find a U.K. labour market uninfluenced by either union or government regulation and whose wages can be compared with those of unionists.

The arbitrary nature of market classifications constitutes a further problem. Most research on differentials implicitly assumes that labour markets function independently, but this is rarely the case. Aggressive trade unions may obtain higher wages not only for their own members but for other groups, if non-union employers match union wage gains to prevent the organisation of their workforce. Where union increases spread to other workers it becomes difficult to isolate their impact on wage differentials; indeed, unionists' wages could be raised by the unionisation of closely related sections of the labour force. The transmission of union gains may become institutionalised in a 'key group' wage pattern, particularly in the United Kingdom, where many unions negotiate in different industries and try to secure equivalent increases in each. Trade-union rhetoric emphasises concepts of 'justice' against those of the market, and Rehn (1957) argued that this emphasis reduces the likelihood of changes in the wage structure based solely on differential power. For these reasons wage gains secured by the strongest groups tend to be 'generalised'.

Because of the pitfalls involved in measuring union influence upon wage differentials, no precise estimate is possible. Controversies of interpretation are inevitable since the relative strength of unions is rarely the sole differentiating factor between markets, but the weight of evidence is sufficiently strong to lend probability to certain conclusions.

THE EVIDENCE

The Initial Impact of Trade Unions

Our analysis predicts that the creation of an effective union permits a permanent, 'once-for-all' increase in its members' wages by eliminating some of the employers' bargaining advantages. This prediction is confirmed by U.S. evidence that during the interwar and immediate post-war years unionisation had an initial impact on relative wages but did not produce a continuous widening of differentials. Lewis (1963) found that the relative wage effect of U.S. trade unions was greatest in the 1930s, when the rapid extension of unionism under the New Deal dissolved many monopsonistic markets and enabled wages to increase at the expense of profits.

The subsequent relative wage effects of unions are harder to isolate. The weight of evidence from U.S. research suggests that some association exists between wage differentials and union strength but a causal connection is difficult to prove. There is reason to believe that unions exert a different impact upon different types of differential, so that each type must be considered separately.

Personal Differentials

Most observers agree that trade unions help to narrow, and sometimes eliminate, personal differentials.[6] In addition they seek to regulate those that remain, e.g. by formalising piece rates, seniority increments and bonus systems. Due to the ease of comparing the wages of individuals doing the same work, unions are under considerable pressure to remove discriminatory personal differentials that may create friction among their members. The pursuit of equal pay for equal work is a basic principle of 'justice' for most unions and much of their early activity is geared to achieving this goal. If union policy succeeds, it establishes 'a rate for the job' instead of a scatter of rates determined unilaterally by the employer. Employers often acquiesce to these demands to achieve administrative simplicity and industrial peace, though in doing so they sacrifice potential profits arising from discrimination. Government minimum-wage legislation also contributed to narrowing personal differentials. However, differentials persist between individuals divided by sex and race. Ostry (1968) attributed the continuance of a pronounced gap between male and female earnings to the intermittent work habits, promotion barriers and discrimination experienced by women.

Firm Differentials

Sizeable wage differentials between firms in the same product and labour markets tend to exist in the absence of trade-union organisation. Over a long period they have narrowed due to the development of national systems of transport and product competition, but effective unions accelerate the process, because imperfections in unorganised markets often enable employers to obtain sufficient labour at wages below those paid by their competitors. Unions can redistribute income from capitalists to workers by imposing standard rates of wages. Employers' associations frequently support such policies since they remove the possibility of cost competition through wage reductions. Unions tend to achieve greater, rather than complete, wage uniformity between firms in the same industry; equal rates are usually specified in collective bargains, but differences in efficiency and in supply and demand movements create divergences in the earnings levels actually paid. However, by imposing minimum standards that extinguish exceptionally low payments, effective unionisation tends to reduce the wage dispersion that remains.

Geographical Differentials

Research from Australia, West Germany and the United States indicates that geographical differentials have narrowed during the present century. Increased dispersion of manufacturing, smaller pockets of labour supply available from agriculture, minimum-wage legislation, concentration of production, and periods of full employment, all contributed to this process, but earnings still differ between areas in response to variations in living costs, the abundance of manpower and the quality of workers. Where union membership is concentrated in high-wage regions they may widen differentials, but where it is spread more evenly they tend to produce a narrowing, by extending the application of wage bargains from the district to the industry level. King (1972) argued that the reduction of regional differentials in the United Kingdom during the First World War was largely due to an increase in union strength[7] which prevented the payment of wages below the competitive level to workers in isolated areas. A combination of three motives – egalitarian philosophy ('equal pay for equal work'), pressure from the low paid and fear of redundancy – has impelled unions to contribute to a process of narrowing geographical differentials that was occurring in response to other influences.

Occupational Differentials

Routh (1965) discovered a narrowing of around 9 per cent in the differential between skilled and unskilled manual workers in the United Kingdom from 1913–14 to 1960. This change was not gradual but was concentrated into the 1913–19 and 1940–50 periods. Skill differentials were fairly constant during the later nineteenth century up to the First World War. Then they declined sharply but were partially restored in the interwar period. The narrowing resumed during the Second World War and its immediate aftermath but did not continue subsequently. The relative gap between manual and non-manual groups was wider in 1960 than in 1913–14 and the ranking of occupations by annual average earnings has barely altered in the twentieth century, except for a significant deterioration in the relative position of the 'lower professions' (a heterogeneous category including school teachers, vets, laboratory assistants and draughtsmen) and of 'clerks'. There is considerable controversy about the causes of these developments, which appear in most industrial countries.

Many argue that unions contributed little to any reduction of occupational differentials because some reduction occurred in countries where unions were weak. During the initial stage of industrialisation occupational differentials widen in response to a scarcity of required skills. Subsequently they narrow as technical change shifts demand away from skilled craftsmen towards semi-skilled machine operators, while the spread of educational provision increases the potential supply of skilled workers. Conversely the proportion of the workforce seeking unskilled jobs falls. Reder (1955) believed that occupational differentials narrow in response to a dilution in employers' hiring standards at full employment. In a slump unemployment is most severe among the unskilled, so that downward pressure on their wages is greatest.

Turner (1957) argued that the wage policy of mass trade unions led to some of the narrowing that did occur; they demanded equal increases for all their members, usually in flat-rate terms, since this method is most attractive to the lower-paid, less-skilled workers who form a majority of their membership.[8] Thus every wage demand of the Confederation of Shipbuilding and Engineering Unions from 1917 to 1952 was for a uniform cash advance. Employers usually accept the form of union claims and bargain only on their amount. Moreover, in periods of rising prices social justice requires compensatory flat-rate wage increases.

Mulvey and Foster (1976) tested the hypothesis that variations in the occupational coverage of collective agreements influenced relative occupational earnings in the United Kingdom. They found a close association in 1973, when the impact of trade unions on relative gross weekly earnings of full-time adult males was estimated to be approximately 25 per cent. Their research provides support for the view that unions significantly affect the structure of occupational differentials.

The uneven growth of unions by occupation possesses consequences for differentials. In nineteenth-century Britain membership was concentrated among skilled manual workers, so that union pressure was designed to maintain or widen differentials, but the subsequent spread of unionisation to the unskilled led to a greater use of flat-rate increases. On balance trade unions tend to strengthen the influences making for greater wage uniformity between occupations where they bargain jointly for different types of labour, but may have the opposite effect when negotiations for different groups occur separately.

Industrial Differentials

Average industrial wages are affected not only by differentials between industries but also by the method of wage payment, the age and sex composition, the skill mix and the geographical distribution of industry workforces. The industrial wage structure exhibits a high degree of long-run stability in the United Kingdom,[9] West Germany, Japan and the United States, while a United Nations survey (1967) found industry rankings to be similar in most developed countries. Rehn (1957) argued that trade unions were partly responsible for this rigidity because they attempt to diminish the impact of changing market forces by establishing a stable but equitable structure based on 'fair relativities'. A considerable body of research has tried to measure the degree to which unions changed industrial differentials, whether in accord with such an overall policy or with sectorial variations in their bargaining power.

The relationship between the U.S. industrial wage structure and union power, measured by unionisation, was examined in great detail by Lewis (1963). His main conclusions were as follows:

(i) Most workers are employed in industries where the union effect on average relative wages is no more than 4 per cent, though for a small minority, including coal-mining, building and hairdressing in some cities, it may be above 20 per cent.

(ii) The average relative wage impact of trade unions varied over time; from 15–20 per cent in 1923–9 to approximately 25 per cent in 1932–3, 10–20 per cent at the end of the 1930s, 0–5 per cent around 1947–8 and 10–15 per cent in the 1950s. As union membership constituted just under a quarter of the work-force in the 1950s, an average wage for unionists 7–11 per cent higher than in the absence of unions is implied, while that of non-unionists would be approximately 3–4 per cent lower.

(iii) Unions raised relative wages most in industries where average wages were already high, to the extent that they increased wage inequality between industries by 6–10 per cent in 1958.

(iv) Unions may reduce inequality within industries by narrowing personal, firm, geographical or occupational differentials more than they raise it between industries. Lewis believed that unions changed within-industry inequality by no more than 5 per cent, so that they altered relative inequality among all workers by less than 6 per cent.

A later study by Levinson (1966) concluded that union strength was more closely related to changes in relative wages than were supply and demand movements. Therefore, U.S. trade unions appear to exert a varying impact on industrial differentials, notably by making money wages more inflexible during a depression, but this impact cannot be measured precisely in view of the operation of other factors.

Similar U.K. research is rare because of the problem of constructing satisfactory proxies for union power. Unionisation is difficult to calculate for U.K. industries because of the non-industrial character of most unions. Moreover, since 1945 annual variations in wage changes have been greater than the inter-industry variance in one year, suggesting that the dominant influences upon wage determination were common to all industries.

However, recent attempts have been made to discover whether industries with relatively strong unions pay greater earnings, *ceteris paribus*, than poorly organised trades. The results are conflicting. Pencavel (1974) estimated a union differential over twenty-nine industries of 0–10 per cent in 1964, while Mulvey (1976) found that the proportion of male workers whose wages were subject to a collective agreement was significantly and positively associated with weekly earnings. When Wabe and Leech (1978) refined the data to allow for the ratio of semi- and unskilled, as well as skilled, workers, they failed to discover any union influence upon the inter-industry variation of average hourly earnings. The U.K. verdict therefore remains unproven. On theoretical grounds, however, any union impact is likely to be less than the 10–15 per cent relative wage

advantage calculated by Lewis (1963) for the United States because
the influence of collective bargaining extends more widely in the
United Kingdom and advantages gained by one group can be
expected to diminish as others orgainise.

The Total Union Impact on Differentials

Trade unions appear to generate a different wage structure from that
prevailing in unorganised markets. They narrow differentials be⁴
tween individuals and firms, and contribute to a secular process of
smaller geographical differentials. Empirical studies of the union
impact on occupational and industrial differentials yield conflicting
results and so must be regarded as inconclusive. When we consider
the varied objectives of unions, the many dimensions of their power
and the shortcomings of conventional measures of objectives (wage
rates) and power (unionisation), the limited nature of past studies
becomes apparent. Future research should take into account the
whole range of living-standard components over which unions bargain and also the many facets of union power essential to the successful pursuit of their objectives. Only analysis that reflects such multi-
dimensionality can advance the argument beyond its present stage.

THE EFFECT OF TRADE UNIONS UPON THE ALLOCATION OF
RESOURCES

If trade unions change wage differentials, they indirectly affect the
allocation of resources. The outcome depends upon the character of
unorganised labour markets.

Rees (1963) developed a theory, illustrated in Figure 3.2, of union
effects upon manpower distribution on the assumption of perfect
competition in the absence of trade unions. Before union development a uniform wage W_o is paid in all labour markets. An effective
union increases this to W_i in sector i, where employment falls from
M_{oi} to M_i. The displaced workers swell the number of job-seekers in
the non-union sector, where employment rises from M_{oj} to M_j, total
employment remaining constant at M. The non-union wage falls from
W_o to W_j. Union wage gains in one sector thus imply relative reductions elsewhere. The demand curves reflect the value of labour's
marginal product under perfect competition, with the areas under
them approximating to the total product. The union-induced redistribution of manpower results in a loss of output in the union sector of

$ACM_{oi}M_i$ while the gain in the non-union sector is EGM_jM_{oj}. Where D_i and D_j possess equal elasticities, triangles ABC and EFG and rectangles $KLM_{oi}M_i$ and FGM_jM_{oj} are congruent. The rectangle $BCKL$ represents the only difference between union-induced gross output gains and losses, and illustrates the net loss. The union wage gain worsens the allocation of resources, as it reduces total output.

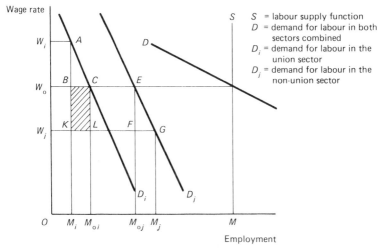

Figure 3.2

Differential elasticities involve different consequences. Workers employed in both industries gain with inelastic demand in the organised, and elastic demand in the unorganised, market. Although those displaced from the unionised industry suffer financial loss, the wage bill in each trade is higher. Aggregate wages in both sectors decrease, if demand is elastic in the organised, and inelastic in the unorganised, industry; with unit elasticity in both a constant labour income is redistributed. Such analysis can be extended to more than two groups with varying degrees of bargaining power, so that trade unions reallocate resources on the basis of the elasticity of demand for labour in each industry and the degree of pressure they can exert.

However, the discussion in Chapter 2 suggests that inherent imperfections of unorganised labour markets enable employers to attract an adequate labour supply at less than competitive wages. Unions may change resource allocation towards the perfectly competitive equilibrium by alleviating the bargaining weakness of individual workers and reducing wage dispersion through the application of standard rates. Ignorance, immobility, unemployment, the existence of non-competing groups and inequality of bargaining power create imperfections that unions help to overcome. Therefore, union wage policy often aids the smooth operation of labour markets. The applicability of Rees's analysis is further lessened by the existence of any spillover of union gains to non-unionists.

CONCLUSION

Under certain circumstances trade unions alter the pattern of wage differentials by overcoming the bargaining weakness of individual workers. The weight of evidence confirms the existence of a significant union impact upon personal, firm and geographical differentials, but union effects upon occupational and industrial differentials remain unclear. Definitions and measurement of 'wages' and 'power' are contentious; results are sensitive to specification, and scope for conflicting interpretations is great. Much confusion has arisen from conventional theories of union behaviour which regard 'power' as an alternative and independent influence from market forces rather than as a multi-dimensional concept comprising and harnessing supply and demand phenomena.

A more fundamental problem remains. Although trade unions are a product of market imperfections and attempt to exploit supply and demand trends favourable to their members, they do not function in the long run within given constraints. They try to change the parameters within which they operate. Their overall long-term objective is to control the job environment, so that a successful application of union power need not show up in a statistical analysis of wages only. Consequently the indecisive empirical evidence concerning union impact upon occupational and industrial differentials is unsurprising. The whole collective bargain, not just wage regulation, requires analysis, so that any theory of relative wages becomes rooted in the dynamics of the use of labour in the production process; thus the stratification of manpower through job hierarchies helps to structure the pattern of differentials. It is in this directions that future advances in understanding must be sought, and in Chapter 6 we consider the non-wage aspects of union activity.

4

Trade Unions and Wage Inflation

INTRODUCTION

Inflation occurs when the general price level increases continuously. It is therefore a monetary phenomenon, and some economists argue that its origins are monetary also. Prior to the so-called 'Keynesian revolution' this was the consensus view, and it held that the supply of money determined the general level of prices. On the assumption of a perfectly competitive labour market, neoclassical theory predicted that money wages adjust to the predetermined price level so as to produce the real wage which equates the supply of and the demand for labour. Keynesian theory, employing different behavioural assumptions, predicts that the general price level and the rate of unemployment are determined by the interaction of the monetary and the real sectors; a key assumption in deriving this prediction is that money wages do not adapt passively to the level indicated by the perfect-competition model, which is an unsuitable theoretical basis for analysing the operation of labour markets. Employers usually possess bargaining advantages when negotiating with individual workmen and so enjoy some degree of control over wage determination. Workers respond by organising trade unions to offset the employers' power through collective action. Neither the employer-dominated unorganised market nor the subsequent development of bargaining institutions resembles the model of perfect competition.

These considerations lead to analyses of inflation that emphasise the behaviour of the money-wage level; thus Kahn (1977) argued that 'Keynesians regard a rapid increase in money wages as the main factor responsible for inflation'. From such a perspective attention is focused upon the role of trade unions in influencing money wages. Workers are paid in money so that they can buy the products of many firms, but their real wages depends upon the prices of these products. No single trade union can increase the real income of its members by controlling prices; consequently it must push up money wages to achieve its objective. This chapter is not designed to provide a comprehensive survey of the process of inflation but focuses upon the issue of whether autonomous union pressure upon the money-wage level can initiate an inflationary spiral of prices and income.

DEMAND-PULL INFLATION

Analyses of inflation refer to demand-pull and to cost-push mechanisms. These are not so much different theories of inflation as different 'schools of thought' within which a number of distinct positions exist.

The only possible source of inflationary pressure in an economy of universal perfect competition would be an increase in purchasing power beyond the level at which such an increase stimulates extra production. Demand-pull theories emphasise the role of excess demand in causing an increase in prices and wages. It is assumed that the aggregate supply function becomes completely inelastic in the short run at the real-income level corresponding to full employment (Y_1 in Figure 4.1). Consequently any increase in demand beyond D_1

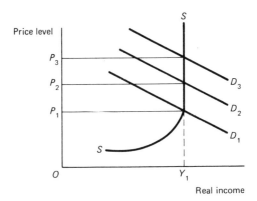

Figure 4.1

causes an upward movement of the general price level, which is not accompanied by a rise in output. This explanation assumes that prices of goods are flexible and are adjusted to excess demand. A rise in the price level occurs when:

$$\frac{D_G - S_G}{S_G} > 0 \qquad (4.1)$$

and a rise in money wages occurs when:

$$\frac{D_L - S_L}{S_L} > 0 \tag{4.2}$$

where D refers to demand, S to available supply, and the subscripts G and L to the goods and labour markets respectively.

In demand-pull theories the speed of wage inflation is determined by the size of excess demand for labour; the trade-off between these variables is reflected in the 'Phillips curve', an empirical attempt to explain and predict the rate of change of money wages from the level and rate of change of unemployment. The weight of evidence suggests that there is a significant relation between money-wage movements and unemployment over very short periods but that the parameters of this relation change with time. Certainly the existence of a long-run trade-off between wage inflation and excess demand remains unsubstantiated.

It is consistent with the demand-pull approach for individual prices to be related to costs, since any change in aggregate demand falls initially upon specific sectors; sectoral increases in demand are transmitted to other industries through a rise in costs. The trade-union role in such a process is confined to obtaining the money-wage increases permitted by the level of excess demand in each labour market. The behavioural relationships underlying demand-pull analysis are essentially atomistic and competitive market processes, described in an abstract sense by the model of perfect competition.

MONETARISM

Trade unions are also assigned a secondary role in the theories of inflation collectively described as 'monetarism'. In their simplest form these assert that increases in the money supply cause increases in prices. The possible effect of money-supply changes upon interest rates and real income is incorporated into more sophisticated versions which hold that the rate of inflation is determined by excess demand and price expectations. The essence of monetarist theories can, at the risk of some simplification, be illustrated by the following identity:

> change in money supply for a closed economy or in domestic credit expansion for an open economy = public sector

borrowing requirement (PSBR) — sales of public-sector
debt to private sector + bank lending to private sector

In this framework excessive monetary growth must be caused by an
excessive PSBR, by inadequate sales of debt to the private sector, by
excessive bank lending to the private sector, or by some combination
of the three. Such approaches have aroused considerable controversy
over the last decade but a detailed analysis is beyond the scope of this
book.[1] Our concern is to consider the significance of monetarism for
an assessment of the role of trade unions in the inflationary process.

Monetarists attribute the continuance and acceleration of inflation
since the Korean war to attempts to keep the level of unemployment
below a 'natural' rate towards which the economy adjusts. The
natural rate is that at which the expected speed of inflation is equal to
its actual speed; consequently it generates a constant rate of price
increase and is consistent with equilibrium in the structure of real
wages. The numerical value of the natural rate at any time is determined by underlying economic forces, such as the speed of industrial
change, labour mobility, trade-union policy and monopolistic restrictions. This concept implies the existence of voluntary unemployment,
as some potential employees prefer not to work at the existing
real-wage level.

Whenever governments attempt to lower unemployment below its
natural rate by increasing the money supply, competitive pressures in
the labour market cause a rise in money wages. In order to preserve
profit margins prices are increased, and this increase is built into
future wage claims, so that inflation accelerates further. Monetarists
believe that inflation can be cured by an adjustment of the money
supply which raises unemployment to its natural level (and even
above, if workers' expectations of future price increases are large).
The current rise of money wages despite growing unemployment
indicates the need for further deflation until the (higher) unemployment level is reached at which inflation is eliminated. In this analysis
full-employment policy no longer centres on aggregate-demand
management but attempts to reduce voluntary and frictional unemployment by sharpening the incentive to work (e.g. through a reduction in unemployment benefit) and by improving information and
mobility in the labour market.

Monetarists accept that some trade unions secure advantages for
their members but see this phenomenon as an isolated exercise of

monopoly power by specific groups which may affect the pattern of relative wages but cannot initiate continuing inflationary pressure. If the union movement as a whole strengthens its bargaining position, a new equilibrium is attained involving a higher real-wage level and a greater natural rate of unemployment. At worst unions could provoke a once-for-all rise in prices if the government pursues an expansionist monetary policy, but monetarists reject the idea that persistent pressure for higher wages leads to a prices–incomes spiral with no equilibrating mechanism.

Our inquiry into the role of trade unions during an inflation cannot stop at this point because certain ambiguities are involved in the monetarist position. Most economists agree that the historically high levels of employment prevailing between 1940 and 1970 were related in some way to inflation, but the direction of causation and its method of operation are subjects of controversy. There are five major objections to monetarist theories:

(i) It is difficult to distinguish empirically whether an increase in the supply of money is a cause or consequence of inflation. Despite the stable velocity of circulation discovered in many econometric studies, it can be argued that the level of economic activity is the independent variable in any casual relationship with the money supply.[2] On this reasoning changes in the demand for money invoke changes in its supply. A number of tests have been carried out that make discrimination possible on this point but not with sufficient clarity to refute either of the alternative hypotheses.

(ii) Monetarism assumes implicitly the existence of atomistic market-clearing processes, but such an assumption is inconsistent with certain observed facts; for instance, the prevalence of collective bargaining, and in its absence government regulation, in the labour market suggests that wage rates are more than merely the price of labour. The existence of rigid structures of wage differentials supports such a view and implies that collective bargaining institutes wage norms relevant to most workers. If this is the case, competitive forces are superseded and wage changes occur more or less independently of the balance between the supply of and the demand for labour in specific markets.

(iii) Difficulties arise in the practical interpretation of the natural rate of unemployment. The latter is unobservable; we could only ascertain its relation to existing unemployment by discovering whether the actual speed of inflation is above or below its expected speed. Since we do not know the expected speed of inflation, neither can we know the natural rate of unemployment, which becomes a tautology. The calculations of Gray, Parkin and Sumner (1975) implied that the natural rate has risen considerably since the mid-1960s in the United Kingdom, from under 2 per cent to nearly 4 per cent. Monetarists explain this increase by the more generous redundancy and unemployment benefits and the spread of minimum-wage legislation, though such explanations are not confirmed by empirical studies of intentions of the unemployed and of the occupational structure of recorded vacancies and unemployment.[3] Moreover, Gray, Parkin and Sumner argued that accelerating inflation was due to the rise in the natural rate, so that the cause of inflation is seen as the extension of social-security provision rather than monetary expansion.

(iv) There is no guarantee that the non-inflationary level of unemployment has acceptable consequences for economic growth, job security and social harmony. If it does not, an awkward political choice arises between full employment and faster growth on the one hand, or lower inflation on the other. Monetarists argue that such a choice is empty and that their policies are the only ones available that are coherent in the long run. However, even if contractionary monetary policies reduce, or even eliminate, price increases, a heavy cost is incurred in terms of low production, unemployment and a check to the improvement of living standards. Recovery from a deep recession tends to be slow due to the loss of business confidence.

(v) Monetarists link monetary expansion to the increased role of governments since 1940 and their commitment to full employment but little explanation is provided of the motives which led to the extension of state economic activity and the adoption of Keynesian policies. Without such analysis the association between inflation, an expansion of the money supply and government policy remains superficial. If government expenditure, in response to workers' pressure for improved social services, leads to an increase in the supply of money, and thereby produces inflation, logically a persistent trade-union push for higher wages could create an identical effect. Skidelsky (1977) argued that if governments could control the money supply at their wish, they would already have done so.

Most economists concede that an expansion of the money supply or of price expectations may precipitate inflation, but they see these as two possible causes among many. An adequate analysis of such a pervasive phenomenon as the post-war inflation must be related to the fundamental dynamic and the historical development of the mixed economy. Within such a perspective inflation becomes the outcome of a struggle over income distribution, the study of which leads to the second inflationary mechanism; increases in costs.

COST-PUSH INFLATION

Cost-push analysis is based on the assumptions that the economy is not perfectly competitive and that organised groups attempt to secure a higher share of real national income by manipulating the money prices over which they exert influence. The mechanism causing prices to rise from an initially stable level is a redistribution of real income unsatisfactory to certain groups, or an attempt by one group to raise its share at others' expense. This can be illustrated by an upward movement of the aggregate supply curve; in Figure 4.2 aggregate supply increases from S_1 to S_2 to S_3, so that full-employment real income (Y_1) can be maintained only by a rising price level (P_1 to P_2 to P_3). If the government attempts to hold prices closer to P_1 by preventing any increase of demand beyond D_1, unemployment results and real income falls to Y_2 and Y_3, while there is still some rise in prices.

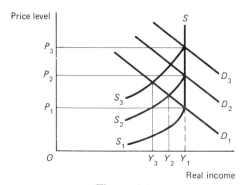

Figure 4.2

Such a situation can occur once the framework of a perfectly competitive economy is abandoned, because the possession of bargaining power enables suppliers of commodities and productive resources to extract higher prices even at the cost of lower sales and employment. A notable example of this ability was the policy of General Motors and its U.S. rivals in 1974, when they raised prices per vehicle by approximately $1000, though sales had fallen to their lowest level in two decades. Whenever a small number of corporations dominate an industry, they can choose between alternative combinations of high prices and small sales or low prices and larger sales. Strong trade unions often enjoy similar discretion in a choice of higher wages and fewer jobs or lower wages and more jobs. Markets for services are not exempt from seller domination; for instance, until the recent Supreme Court rebuke, U.S. lawyers circulated minimum-fee schedules to protect themselves from price competition.

Under oligopoly a change in costs leads, after a varying time lag, to a change in prices. In a regime of market imperfections and administered prices, income movements may be self-financing; if a general increase in money wages occurs at an equilibrium market position, industry supply schedules, and thus aggregate supply, move to the left as the marginal-cost curves of individual firms rise. However, the higher wages increase aggregate demand also (from D_1 to D_2 to D_3 in Figure 4.2), so that a new price–output equilibrium is reached. Because a money-wage change implies an upward movement of both aggregate supply and aggregate demand, the general price level is not uniquely determined by their equality, and equilibrium can be attained at any level of money wages and prices. There is no guarantee that the sum of successful claims for higher money incomes will be equal to productive potential; if it is greater, inflation results.

Therefore, cost-push inflation may arise when productive groups charge a higher price for their services. This can occur in the labour market, which is inherently imperfect and occupies such a prominent place in the economy that general increases in money wages and salaries may create the additional demand required to sustain them. Such a possibility becomes more likely with the tendency for employers to bargain as a group. One firm cannot grant wage claims and be confident of recouping them through higher prices, but if all firms in an industry face the same scale of cost increases, they tend to raise prices by a similar amount. No single firm risks losing custom to its competitors and their resistance to wage claims weakens as they realise that cost increases can be passed on to consumers without incurring financial loss. Under these conditions wage movements do not depend, as Laidler (1975) argued, solely on the immediate level of demand and expectations of future price changes.

The struggle of groups to maintain, and if possible increase, their real income by raising money incomes is likely to intensify as full employment is approached. If output cannot expand, greater money incomes cause increased prices, and only when all groups stop attempting to increase their share of income will costs and prices cease to rise. This may occur when those living on fixed incomes sustain sufficient losses through rising prices to satisfy the real-income demands of other classes, or when the pace of inflation accelerates so quickly that it provokes a government counter policy severe enough to curtail claims for higher incomes.

Figure 4.3 illustrates the situation in which the intensity of cost-push forces is related to aggregate demand, since the extent of a shift in supply (i.e. from S_1 to S_2 and from S_2 to S_3) tends to increase with a fall in unemployment. Both cost and demand forces can initiate an inflation and frequently they interact.

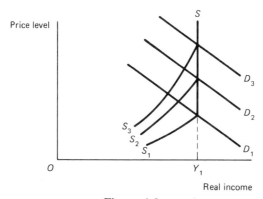

Figure 4.3

THE PRICES–INCOMES SPIRAL

An initial demand-pull or cost-push impetus may trigger an inflationary spiral in which prices and incomes chase each other upwards. Brown (1955) argued that a prices–incomes spiral operates when income changes become closely correlated with movements in the cost of living. Whether price or income changes 'start' the process is irrelevant, because no originally 'fair' distribution between wages and profits exists. Consequently any change can be seen as a disturbance or a just correction depending on the observer's opinion. As an increase in money income tends to generate a more or less proportional price rise, the expected real income level is not achieved. Another round of income claims begins and this interaction can continue indefinitely.

As price increases become cost increases for both individual and industrial customers, the spiral has its own dynamic at or near full employment. Capitalists and workers may seek more than compensation for their loss since the last 'round' so that a further acceleration occurs. The essence of a prices–incomes spiral lies in the reaction of capitalists to demand and cost changes and of workers to movements in living standards.

THE SOURCES OF COST-PUSH INFLATION IN THE LABOUR MARKET

Trade unions participate in collective bargaining in order to maintain and improve their members' real incomes and conditions of work. Although inflation can originate from other productive resources, many economists[4] have argued in recent years that union policies to achieve these ends generate an inflationary bias, so that the relationship between wage increases and excess demand differs under collective bargaining from that which would prevail in an unorganised labour market. The latter is assumed to have a wage-adjustment function as in equation (4.3), while the unionised market is assumed to possess an adjustment function as in equation (4.4), so that:

$$\Delta W_t = a \left\{ \frac{D_L - S_L}{S_L} \right\}_t \qquad (4.3)$$

$$\Delta W_t = b \left\{ \frac{D_L - S_L}{S_L} \right\}_t + c \qquad (4.4)$$

where ΔW is the rate of change of money wages, D_L is the level of demand for labour, S_L is the level of supply of labour, t is the current year, and a, b and c are positive parameters.

Figure 4.4 illustrates possible adjustment functions. AA plots the unorganised market function showing that when excess demand is zero ΔW will be zero. BB represents a possible unionised adjustment function such that when excess demand is zero a constant rate of wage inflation (OX) occurs, and ΔW becomes nil only with excess labour supply (OY). The position of BB implies that trade unions generate a greater rate of money-wage increase at each level of excess demand, while the increasing gap between BB and AA indicates that the extent of union-induced wage gains rises with a fall in unemployment. The latter proposition is intuitively plausible but its truth does not affect the validity of the major hypothesis of the relationship between wage inflation and trade-union bargaining power.

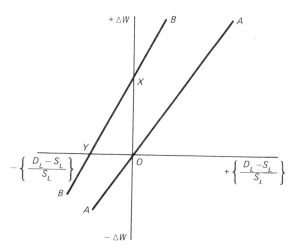

Figure 4.4

We believe that whatever the precise direction of BB above AA union activities can be a source of cost-push inflation under present socio-economic conditions. Current economic problems must be viewed against their social background, since inflation emerges in the form of a wage push as the result of deep-rooted social conflicts. The factors promoting such conflict must be considered in detail in any analysis of recent inflationary experience.

The Economic Implications of Full Employment

The most important development promoting intensified trade-union wage push was the maintenance of full employment between 1940 and 1970. In a capitalist economy the bargaining strength of unions is usually small in comparison with that of employers, but a long period of continuous full employment causes a shift in the balance of power. Union sanctions impose heavier costs upon employers when demand is high, since any interruption to production causes a decline in sales and eventually in profits. Even for a firm close to bankruptcy or operating on a tight cash flow, the cost of a strike may be greater than the cost of concession. Employers experience difficulty in recruiting labour, so that failure to increase wages may lead to a loss of the most efficient workers or damage their morale. Wage claims become easier to grant when firms realise that they can be passed on in higher prices. On the other hand, strikers incur fewer risks at full employment, because the supply of unemployed labour capable of replacing them is negligible, and possible employer reactions such as dismissal or a blacklist lose much of their coercive potential when workers who lose a job feel that they can easily obtain another. Until 1940 trade unions faced the continual threat, and the periodic occurrence, of unemployment; only since then have they negotiated free from the constraints placed upon them by the possibility of mass redundancy. Consequently they are in a stronger position to press claims, while employers possess less incentive to resist.

The Social Implications of Full Employment

The maintenance of full employment involves profound consequences for social relations. Workers who become unemployed usually obtain another job quickly, so that their dependence on a particular employer lessens. The threat of dismissal loses much of its force and industrial discipline is correspondingly harder to maintain. Part of the employers' social superiority and the need for workers' servility disappears, resulting in a fundamental change in the character of the capital–labour relationship. Subordination and deference become less acceptable, and a powerful sanction preventing militancy is removed. This growth in working-class self-assurance finds its most available outlet in pressure for money-wage increases. Full employment does not eliminate conflict over the distribution of income but by enabling workers to strive less inhibitedly for higher money wages it tends to produce rising costs and prices, unless its effects are modified by changes in economic institutions.

The Political Implications of Full Employment

The likelihood of cost-push inflation is increased by a government commitment to maintain full employment. With the existence of such a commitment trade unions often behave as though the demand for labour is highly inelastic over a widening range of wage rates. Unionists believe that departures from full employment are electorally damaging, so that any unemployment due to higher wages is soon mitigated by government management of demand. Post-war experience showed that rises in pay which had been resisted as financially injurious were in fact compatible with the maintenance of full employment and a progressive increase in living standards. Restraints on future pay claims were thereby weakened. Moreover, political competition for votes might create inflation, as in the U.K. pre-election booms of 1959 and 1964. Wage demands in these circumstances become increasingly insistent, while employers find that higher cost and price structures are supported by government policy.

The Greater Political Power of the Union Movement

The relationship between governments and the trade-union movement has changed drastically since the 1930s, partly because of full employment but even more because of the effects of the United Kingdom's weakened economic position, which has led all governments to rely at least tacitly on union co-operation. This does not imply that unions can often impose their will upon governments but they are involved closely in state administration and possess some influence over the process of decision-making. The stronger position of the Labour Party, with which U.K. unions are closely identified, also contributed to the greater political power enjoyed by organised workers since 1945.

Increasing Monopoly Power

The increasing size and market power of many firms arising from economies of large-scale production enable them to control their own prices. They do not release their product on to the market to see what it will fetch but announce the price at which they are prepared to sell. Oligopolists dare not risk price increases unless competitors are likely to follow their example; a rise in labour costs common to all firms in an industry often provides a suitable occasion for a price increase. Therefore, oligopolistic prices tend to be rigid in relation to demand but highly responsive to cost changes. The strength of non-price competition in imperfect markets gives producers a powerful incentive to prevent strikes in order to retain their distributive networks and their market share. Such attitudes are intensified by the enormous capital investments that large firms undertake while still relying on labour for continuous-flow production. The increased centralisation and integration of manufacturing enables groups of workers, often small in number, to close down a firm or even an industry. Under these conditions strikes involve heavy costs, and highly capitalised firms make considerable concessions to avoid them.

Price Expectations

The maintenance of full employment over a long period changes expectations in a way conducive to the acceleration of inflation. Workers' living standards grow when money wages increase more rapidly than the cost of living, but prices rise between pay settlements, so that anticipated gains are eroded and a powerful motive behind the next claim is to restore the previous level of real income. Arguments that wage increases cause prices to rise do not convince the individual worker, since almost all the higher prices he has to meet originate in industries unaffected by his own income. Prolonged inflation educates trade-union leaders to bargain in real terms by allowing for expected price movements, so that incomes rapidly adjust to, or even anticipate, changes in the price level. This concentration on real incomes also causes unions to push up money wages to offset the effects of increased indirect taxation upon their members' living standards.

Social Emulation

Two decades of continuous economic growth fostered the expectation of a continued annual improvement. The relative advance of different groups became a matter for concern, as increased car ownership and regular television viewing stimulated an awareness of different ways of life, while improved educational provision enabled more people to question the rationality and justice of existing socioeconomic relations. The advertising industry strengthens such tendencies by inducing workers to seek a style of life which is beyond their means but is enjoyed by other classes. It is unlikely that any attainable level of real income satisfies for long those whose material aspirations are constantly stimulated in an unequal society. In these circumstances discontent arises from the gap between one's existing conditions and those that others enjoy. The motive power of economic progress under capitalism depends largely upon the urge to satisfy such relative needs, so that claims on resources exceed productive capacity in a period of continuous full employment when such claims can be pressed. The resulting social and economic tensions generate cost-push inflation.

Wage Bargaining by Sectors

The tendency to social emulation is strengthened by the practice of negotiating wages separately in each industry. The U.K. tradition of independent sectoral bargaining, with relatively weak central employer and union organisations and strong resistance to government intervention, makes a common union policy difficult to achieve because it is incompatible with the attempt of each trade union to establish a bargaining position from which it can extract the highest possible money wage. Union development occurred segmentarily (craft, industrial, general unions, etc.), and sometimes tactics and interests clash. Union power has been increasingly decentralised since the 1940s; even where individual-plant bargains are beneficial for the workers involved, they are by their nature piecemeal and often based on unrelated or divergent principles which breed conflict between employers and workers and among the workforce.

Unco-ordinated union policies create the phenomena of wage leadership and wage generalisation. Each union's success improves its members' relative position and stimulates other unions to restore differentials. Any disturbance of traditional relativities gives rise to attempts to restore them; for instance, if productivity increases rapidly in one industry so that higher wages are paid, present attitudes refuse to tolerate a smaller rise in living standards in other industries. This is not irrational, for many jobs (particularly in services) have little scope to increase productivity and even in manufacturing productivity growth is due less to workers' efforts than to investment programmes. If workers in fast-growth sectors obtain a wage rise equal to the growth of productivity and this increase becomes generalised to other industries, unit costs increase and rising prices result. Wages are viewed by their recipients partly as a source of purchasing power and partly as an index of social status. This dual role implies that wage comparisons between groups create a situation in which any disturbance of the pay structure leads to inflationary attempts to restore relative status.

Sectoral bargaining places each trade union in a 'prisoner's dilemma'. If a union moderates its wage claims in order to help curtail inflation, it imposes a relative loss upon its members if other unions proceed as before. Only if the whole union movement adopts a co-ordinated policy can it negotiate the real rather than the monetary value of wages and thus mitigate a source of inflationary pressure.

Political Equality

Under a democracy based on universal suffrage political rights are nominally equal and workers may attempt to extend such rights to economic matters. The welfare state, which aimed to establish a minimum income for all, was the first stage in this process; the subsequent step in an age of rising living standards is the effort of specific groups to climb the income pyramid. The concept of 'relative deprivation' is based on comparisons and is equally as likely to occur in an affluent as in an impoverished society. If one group improves its relative position, others lose, so that a quest for equity can initiate a wage–wage spiral.

Social-security Provision

More liberal unemployment benefits have lessened the fear of any redundancies that might result from wage increases, while long strikes have been made easier to conduct by the provision of social-security benefits for the families of strikers. Economists like Haberler (1972) place great emphasis on these developments but they seem more a manifestation of social change then its cause.

Devaluation

Haberler (1972) also argued that the diversion of U.K. products away from the domestic market to exports and the higher cost of imports after the 1967 devaluation led to a temporary reduction in living standards and hence to an intensified push for wage increases. The downward 'float' of sterling since 1971 exerted a similar effect.

Conclusion

The interaction of these developments has strengthened the operation of cost-push forces in the United Kingdom since 1940. Continuous full employment between 1940 and 1970 changed attitudes and relationships in such a way as to intensify claims for higher incomes. Without corresponding modifications in the institutional framework, these changes lead to an upward movement of the aggregate supply curve, which becomes wage-inelastic over a range of real income levels below that of full employment. The commitment of classes to their existing living standards causes them to increase their money incomes in an attempt to maintain real income when prices rise. If they fail, their standard of living falls and ultimately the size of the group is lowered, but this occurs only after political and economic struggle. If they succeed, a prices–incomes spiral is initiated which ceases only when each group's desired expenditure equals its possible expenditure. Some 'normal' gap between the two is usually sufficient for social equilibrium to be attained. This gap is reached by a change in output consequent upon a change in demand, by a change in the size of social groups, or by a change in consumption habits or living standards. The experience of over a generation of price increases developed inflationary expectations that gave added momentum to the process of cost-push inflation, in which an increased money supply appears as a permissive but not a causal factor.

It is sometimes claimed that socio-economic analyses fail to explain the acceleration of inflation from 1968. However, Phelps Brown (1975) argued that this acceleration was related to the changing composition of the labour force. The persistence of attitudes inculcated during the interwar depression, when job security was workers' major concern, constituted a check to any pay explosion in the twenty years after 1945. Every year workers with this background retired to be replaced by those whose experience was confined to full-employment conditions which provided a measure of independence from the employer. By 1968 only a quarter of U.K. employees had been members of the work-force before 1939. Gradually the proportion with solely post-war memories became predominant and sufficient to outweigh tradition and the respect granted to older men.

Their outlook did not accept the necessity for wage restraint to preserve jobs, so that the forces analysed above gathered momentum.

THE EMPIRICAL EVIDENCE

Attempts have been made to assess whether the variability of the rate of inflation over time was associated with changes in trade-union bargaining power. They yield a series of conflicting results, partly because of differences in the specification of the models and of the variables. The lack of a theoretical basis for much of the research tends to produce mis-specifications, while reliable conclusions are unlikely to be established within a theoretical vacuum. Moreover, the concept of union bargaining power is multi-dimensional, so that attempts to measure it are at best rough approximations.

Hines (1964) produced econometric evidence that the rate of change of unionisation was a significant explanatory variable of the rate of change of money wages in the United Kingdom between 1893 and 1961. He suggested that this relationship reflected trade-union militancy manifested in simultaneous recruitment campaigns and wage claims. Hines's (1964, 1969 and 1971) research prompted considerable discussion, by, for example, Stoney and Thomas (1970), Purdy and Zis (1974), Wilkinson and Burkitt (1973) and Burkitt and Bowers (1976). Subsequent studies indicate that the unionisation model has a lower statistical significance and is subject to greater variation than Hines claimed, but the rate of change of unionisation usually remains significant in the wage-determination equation. The lack of theoretical precision makes it difficult to discriminate between conflicting explanations of this association. Ultimately in the present state of knowledge one's choice of hypothesis is a matter of judgement. Evidence from other Western countries is also inconclusive (see Trevithick and Mulvey, 1975).

At industry level differential union strength may not produce differential wage increases, because trade unions may influence the overall level of money wages while maintaining a stable wage structure. Criteria of horizontal and vertical equity can generalise the advances in living standards gained by one industry to other sectors. Much U.K. and U.S. research verifies the existence of a wage-transfer process, but the role played by unions requires greater analysis.

The weight of evidence suggests that trade-union bargaining power can effect money-wage movements and introduce an inflationary bias into the labour market. In seeking to maintain their members' real living standards unions escalate the reaction of wages to price changes,[5] while their existence seems to facilitate the generalisation of key wage bargains. The impact of other union activities remains controversial. These conclusions must be assessed in relation to the problems encountered by research in this area, notably the difficulty of constructing sensitive proxies for cost-push forces. It seems unlikely that such a complex socio-economic phenomenon as the modification of relationships during a period of continuous full employment can be analysed by simple econometric techniques.

ARE TRADE UNIONS TO BLAME FOR INFLATION?

The increased strength of cost-push tendencies is due largely to full employment, which strengthens the ability of trade unions to increase money wages. It would be wrong, however, to blame unions for the recent inflation. Despite intensified wage push the privileged members of society continue to exist outside union ranks. Power remains unequally divided, with employers tending to be richer and enjoying greater security. The acceleration of money-wage increases between 1969 and 1973 raised the share of employee compensation (see below, p. 61) in G.N.P by 1.3 per cent. Union claims were not self-defeating but their redistributive impact was hardly substantial. Since unions exercise no direct control over the price level it is in their members' short-term interest to push money wages as high as possible.

Trade unions play an important role in generating inflation yet are unable to achieve a sizeable redistribution of income. Unions do not deserve censure for this state of affairs; since the industrial revolution of the eighteenth and nineteenth centuries the prevailing climate of values has exhorted individuals to display ambition to manoeuvre for higher incomes and to judge success in terms of material rewards. Such values intensified with the post-war growth of conspicuous consumption and the expansion of advertising. Businessmen and professional workers tend to pursue their financial self-interest as individuals, but the weaker bargaining position of manual workers and their lack of promotion opportunities compel them to act as a group to increase living standards (see Chapter 2). Middle-class salaries are often negotiated individually, or for a small number, so that pay increases can be awarded without causing prices to rise. This is a source of advantage during an inflation, when group bargaining on behalf of manual workers inevitably raises the question of its effect upon unit costs. Although very few of the middle or working classes associate their own pay with national economic phenomena, their claims for increases are in practice judged on different criteria, with only those of manual workers being assessed in terms of their effect upon the economy as a whole.

Trade unions are able to pursue their members' financial self-interest with fewer inhibitions than before 1939. When most classes possess sufficient power to act effectively on the philosophy of self-aggrandisement which bolsters our economic system, that system itself is in danger of collapse through the prices–incomes spiral. Greater equality of bargaining power in a changed socio-economic environment enables unions to increase money wages but is insufficient for them to secure fundamental changes in the power structure of society.[6] The resulting inflation poses new and unresolved problems for government economic policy. These problems are analysed in Chapter 7.

CONCLUSION

In an imperfectly competitive economy the determination of factor prices may be substantially independent of the level of aggregate demand and so be influenced by the application of bargaining power. Cost-push inflation can arise when the owners of productive resources in total claim an income which is higher than aggregate output, a situation that becomes more frequent as full employment is approached. Recently cost-push tendencies strengthened in response to changes in economic and social relationships arising out of the maintenance of full employment between 1940 and 1970. No institutional alterations occurred to accommodate the effects of these changes. The result has been a persistent upward movement of the aggregate supply curve. One type of inflation emerges as a wage push instigated by trade unions in response to distributional conflicts in a society of considerable inequality. The search by governments for an effective policy to counter rising prices is likely to modify the character of labour markets and the role of trade unions within them.

5

Trade Unions and the Distribution of Income

INTRODUCTION

The previous analysis suggested that under certain circumstances trade unions possess the ability to increase the wages paid to organised workers relative to those of the unorganised and also to increase the general level of money wages. Little has been said about the movement of wages and salaries compared with changes in other types of income. The behaviour of real wages over a long period depends upon the growth of real income per head and upon the distribution of total income. The present chapter concentrates upon the distribution of income between labour (i.e. the human resources used in production) and property;[1] in any economy this is determined by the interaction between technical conditions and social relationships.

THE POTENTIAL SCOPE FOR TRADE-UNION ACTION TO ALTER THE DISTRIBUTION OF INCOME

Three interrelated phenomena largely determine the distribution of income in the United Kingdom. These are the private ownership of property, the over-all balance and detailed structure of supply and demand in the labour market, and the activity of the state in collecting taxes, distributing benefits and attempting to influence the operation of the economy.[2]

Many supporters of the trade-union movement believe that its major effect has been to raise the share of national income accruing to labour. In any type of economy, given existing techniques of production and the volume of capital equipment, the total wage and salary bill cannot exceed national income in the short run, while over a longer period it is limited to national income minus the funds required to maintain the capital stock. Where a target rate of economic growth is sought a further deduction from potential labour income must be made to permit the necessary volume of net new investment. National income minus these deductions constitutes the maximum labour income consistent with the planned rate of growth, and is the upper limit to union bargaining achievements.

In a capitalist economy labour's share is usually below its potential maximum because property incomes derived from the ownership of productive assets are used not only to maintain and expand the capital stock but also to finance consumption. In a society based upon private ownership of the means of production profit is a necessary cost for inducing capitalists to part with their liquidity and incur the risk of financial loss, so that workers are deprived of the resources devoted to satisfying capitalist consumption. The ability of trade unions to increase labour's share of national income depends upon the extent to which they can reduce capitalist consumption without endangering the growth of the capital stock upon which their members' incomes ultimately rest.

If unions succeed in raising the general level of real wages at full-employment real income, the increase can be maintained only by a reduction in the share of income received by property-owners, who will be compelled to curtail either their consumption or their investment expenditure. If investment is cut, real wages may in the long run fall to a lower level than that prevailing before the increase. The degree to which unions can eat into capitalist consumption on behalf of their members depends upon the spending habits of those owning capital. If their marginal propensity to consume is large, unions can make considerable inroads into capitalist consumption, but if it is small such a feat is unlikely.[3] The probability is that the marginal propensity to consume from property incomes is small, partly because these contain the richest individuals and partly because most profits accrue to companies, which in the main allocate a high proportion to their reserves. Consumption patterns tend to be rigid because a normal degree of luxury based on past experience is widely regarded as an essential charge upon income, with additional increments of purchasing power being diverted increasingly to investment. Capitalists usually attempt to maintain their habitual level of consumption and draw upon savings to resist any reduction. A fall in their incomes is reflected in investment, so that the scope for trade unions to make permanent gains at their expense is limited.

Such a situation arises because of the unequal distribution of wealth. Most people possess only their labour power, while the ownership of finance capital is concentrated into the hands of a relatively small group which makes scarce funds available for the purchase of machinery and plant. Atkinson (1972) found that the richest 1 per cent of the British population own at least one-quarter, and the richest 5 per cent at least one-half, of total personal wealth. The distribution of income from property is even more unequal, with 5 per cent of all adults receiving no less than 92 per cent of all property income and 93 per cent of adults in 1970 owning no shares or government bonds. Although the distribution of wealth and property incomes appears to be more unequal in Britain than in most other developed capitalist economies, a similar pattern emerges elsewhere.

Our argument suggests that trade unions find difficulty in raising labour's share of the national income because only slight inroads into capitalist consumption are possible without reducing the rate of accumulation and, therefore, long-run standards of living. Glyn and Sutcliffe (1972) found that national rankings on the basis of investment and profitability levels were almost identical. However, the national income of most economies has grown over a long period under the impact of more efficient productive techniques. In these circumstances unions possess the opportunity to raise real wages at the expense of a potential increase in capitalist consumption. By pressing for higher wages unions may reduce the growth of capitalist consumption without significantly affecting the expansion of investment. King and Regan (1976) provided evidence that in the United Kingdom the savings propensity of capitalists fluctuated over short periods while increasing secularly in the post-war years. Such an increase may enable a constant level of investment to be financed from a declining profits share (or a higher level of investment from a stable share). Whether these possibilities materialise depends partly upon the strength of trade unions, reflected in their ability to impose costs of disagreement upon employers.

Just as the consumption habits of property-owners place an upper limit on labour's share of the national income, a lower limit is set by the subsistence level of wages. In a developed economy this level is set by traditional and expected consumption standards, which may be raised by union action. Between these extremes a range of possible labour shares exists, through which unions aim to advance by exploiting their bargaining power upon the level of money wages. They cannot push the labour share above this range unless they obtain institutional changes that modify the operation of capitalism, for example the provision of an increasing volume of capital equipment by the state. A less fundamental change would be a rise in the proportion of total savings supplied by labour. Eltis (1973) advocated a wealth tax on the rich coupled with subsidies for savings schemes used by small- and middle-income recipients; union participation in capital-formation funds, discussed by Skinner (1972), also promotes an increase in the worker's propensity to save. Political decisions (e.g. state control of the general price level) can affect the size of the labour share by influencing the positions from which employers and trade unions bargain. Before considering whether unions have increased the proportion of the national income paid to labour we must present the empirical evidence on the behaviour of relative shares.

A REVIEW OF THE EVIDENCE

We follow Feinstein (1968) in dividing national income into the following categories: *wages* (the pay of manual workers), *employee compensation* (wages plus salaries, abbreviated to E.C.), *labour income* (E.C. plus the imputed labour income of the self-employed), *corporate profits, total profits* (corporate profits plus interest and rent) and *property income* (total profits plus the imputed property income of the self-employed). (The series shown in Table 5.1 are derived from Feinstein (1968) and King and Regan (1976), with updating to 1976 by the present authors.)

Table 5.1 reveals a short-run cyclical fluctuation in relative shares. The E.C. share tends to move in a counter-cyclical direction, while that of corporate profits increases in a boom and falls in a recession. These trends arise from the sensitivity of profits to changes in the level of business activity. It is probably true that the same pattern applies to the labour and property shares, with the former rising in slumps and falling in booms and the latter moving in an opposite manner.[4]

It has frequently been argued that over a long period[5] labour's share of the national income remained constant; for example, Keynes (1939) wrote that 'the stability of the proportion of the national dividend accruing to labour is one of the most surprising yet best-

Table 5.1   Income shares as a percentage of gross national product at factor cost: United Kingdom 1860–9 to 1976

| Years | Employee compensation | Income from self-employment | | Corporate profits | Rent | Total domestic profits | Net property income from abroad | Gross national product |
		Farmers	Others					
1860–9	45.2	6.4	30.6		14.8	—	3.0	100
1870–9	45.2	4.5	32.1		13.7	—	4.5	100
1880–9	46.2	2.7	31.4		13.9	—	5.8	100
1890–9	48.0	2.4	30.8		12.5	—	6.2	100
1900–9	47.7	2.3	31.3		12.1	—	6.6	100
1910–14	47.3	2.5	13.7	17.1	11.0	28.1	8.4	100
1921–4	58.5	2.1	15.1	13.0	6.8	19.8	4.5	100
1925–9	58.1	1.3	14.8	12.5	7.5	20.0	5.8	100
1930–4	59.3	1.6	13.4	12.5	9.0	21.5	4.2	100
1935–8	58.9	1.6	11.6	15.0	8.8	23.8	4.1	100
1946–9	65.3	2.9	9.4	16.8	4.0	20.8	1.7	100
1950–4	65.3	2.8	7.8	18.0	3.9	21.9	2.1	100
1955–9	67.0	2.3	6.9	18.0	4.5	22.5	1.3	100
1960–3	67.4	2.1	6.3	17.9	5.1	23.0	1.2	100
1964–8	67.6	8.0		16.8	6.4	23.2	1.2	100
1969–73	68.9	9.0		13.2	7.6	20.8	1.3	100
1974	70.4	10.3		16.9	7.1	23.9	1.7	100
1975	73.1	9.5		13.7	7.1	20.8	1.0	100
1976	71.3	9.3		15.4	7.0	22.5	1.1	100

Note: The above columns sum to more than 100 by 6.3 (1974), 4.3 (1975), 4.1 (1976) due to the residual error of national income accounting. See note 21 of *National Income and Expenditure, 1962– 1972* (London: H.M.S.O., 1973).

Sources: (i) 1860–9 to 1960–3 – Feinstein (1968), table 1, pp. 116– 17, as adapted by King and Regan (1976), table 1, p. 19; (ii) 1964–8 and 1969–73 – King and Regan (1976), table 1, p. 19; (iii) 1974, 1975, 1976 – calculated by the present authors from *National Income and Expenditure* (London, H.M.S.O.) data.

established facts in the whole range of economic statistics'. The wage share alone has not fluctuated greatly in the United Kingdom but the proportion paid in salaries varied more and exhibited a secular tendency to rise. This behaviour implies that the E.C. share rose over the last hundred years, from approximately 45 per cent in the 1860s to over 70 per cent today. The distinction between those paid by wages and those paid by salary is of declining significance. Many wage-earning jobs have been converted into salaried posts, though their character remained unaltered. While Atkinson (1972) found the average wage in 1961 to be approximately three-quarters of the average salary, a sizeable minority of manual workers now earn more than the salary norm. The ranks of the salaried include such occupations as company directors, whose incomes reflect their control over property, but in quantitative terms these are few. Consequently the behaviour of the wage share is less significant than that of employee compensation.

Table 5.2   The distribution of income between labour and property: United Kingdom, 1910–14 to 1976

Years (annual averages)	% of gross national product		% of gross domestic product	
	Labour	Property	Labour	Property
1910–4	55.3	44.7	60.2	39.8
1921–4	67.4	32.6	70.6	29.4
1925–9	66.4	33.6	70.5	29.5
1930–4	68.1	31.9	71.1	28.9
1935–8	67.1	32.9	70.0	30.0
1946–9	73.0	27.0	74.3	25.7
1950–4	72.1	27.9	73.7	26.3
1955–9	73.4	26.6	74.4	25.6
1960–3	73.6	26.4	74.5	25.5
1964–8	73.6	26.4	74.4	25.6
1969–73	75.6	24.4	76.6	23.4
1974	78.1	21.9	79.4	20.6
1975	80.2	19.8	81.0	19.0
1976	78.3	21.7	78.3	21.7

Note: The above calculations impute 75 per cent of self-employment income to labour, and 25 per cent to property.

Sources: (i) 1910–14 to 1960–3 – Feinstein (1968), table 5, p. 126; (ii) 1964–8 and 1969–73 – King and Regan (1976), table 2, p. 20; (iii) 1974, 1975 and 1976 – calculated by the present authors using the data from Table 5.1.

Table 5.2 summarises the long-run trend of income shares, with the income of the self-employed being imputed between labour and property. The estimates can only be tentative because they fail to take account of the distributive impact of taxation and government expenditure. Over the last century the share of labour rose at the expense of property, but this shift was concentrated into three periods: between 1910–14 and 1921–4, between 1935–8 and 1946–9, and from 1968 to 1975. No major changes took place before 1914, between the wars, or from 1950 to 1968.

In almost all developed countries the E.C. share rose as in the United Kingdom (see Kuznets, 1955) but the behaviour of the labour share was less uniform. In the United Kingdom, West Germany and France it increased, and in Sweden it remained constant; in the United States the evidence for the first three decades of this century is conflicting, but most research indicates that it did not rise significantly from the 1930s to the mid-1960s. Since then, on the figures presented by Thirlwall (1972) and Nordhaus (1974), labour has gained at the expense of profits. This conclusion is confirmed by our calculation of U.S. income shares since 1950, contained in Table 5.3.

Therefore, the weight of evidence refutes the hypothesis of a

Table 5.3   Percentage income shares in the United States, 1950 to 1976

Year	Employee com- pensation	Pro- prietors' income	Rental income of persons	Cor- porate profits	Balancing item (net interest)
1950	65.5	16.3	3.0	14.3	0.9
1955	68.6	13.0	3.4	13.6	1.4
1960	71.6	11.4	3.3	11.3	2.4
1965	70.1	10.0	3.0	13.6	3.3
1970	76.3	8.2	2.3	8.5	4.7
1975	76.9	7.5	1.9	7.6	6.1
1976	76.3	7.2	1.7	8.7	6.1

Source: U.S. Department of Commerce, *Statistical Abstract of the United States 1977*, Bureau of the Census, Washington, D.C., published annually, table 697.

long-run constancy in relative shares when the overall labour share rather than that of wages only is the variable studied. In most countries the labour share was higher, and the property share lower, in 1970 than in 1900. The overwhelming majority of this increase in the United Kingdom occurred during three periods: those in and around the world wars and the last decade. Any theory of distribution must explain developments over the years when labour's share tends to stability (abstracting from short-term cyclical fluctuations) and also the forces which lead to the major upward displacements. The trade-union role in each situation requires careful consideration.

PERIODS OF STABILITY

Goodwin (1967) argued that capitalist development tends to maintain a stable relationship between the size of profits and real wages. Cyclical oscillations of output and employment are intimately linked with short-run changes in distribution in such a way as to keep the long-term shares of property and labour approximately constant. If real wages rise at full employment due to market forces or the application of union power, profits fall,[6] so that investment financed from property incomes either declines or rises at a reduced speed, and the creation of new jobs slows down. However, the labour force normally grows in response to natural increase and to the release of individual workers from specific jobs under the impact of technical progress. Thus unemployment rises and excess supply of labour causes wage increases to lag behind productivity growth, though the real-wage level falls absolutely only in a severe depression. Profits rise and capital accumulation accelerates, leading to a growth in output and a reduction in unemployment, with consequent wage increases.

This cycle can continue indefinitely: workers enjoy a persistent but unsteady improvement in their standard of living, yet trade unions exert little effect upon income distribution. Such a model explains the paradox that most unions believe that they can, and indeed have, raised wages at the expense of profits, though the available evidence suggests that changes in income shares have been limited to specific periods. The approximate stability of the labour share over long periods implies a general correspondence between the growth of wages and profitability; technical progress provides a boost to profits, but subsequent expansion of output and employment forces wages up and profits down. Increases in either real wages or profitability at the other's expense create a situation that ensures their temporary character. The operation of this mechanism over periods of many years raises the question of what causes its suspension when labour's share is displaced.

PERIODS OF DISPLACEMENT

Owen Smith (1975) suggested five reasons for the increase in the proportion of national income accruing to labour during the last hundred years. First, the supply of capital and the capital–labour ratio has risen; the effect of this was to lower the relative productivity of capital and hence its share in national income. Second, the number of self-employed declined, so that yesterday's small businessman became today's wage-earner. This factor alone would enable the share of labour to increase relative to that of property, even though income per employee remained constant. Third, the demand for labour increased because technical change tended to be labour-using and also because the structure of employment shifted towards those industries with relatively high proportionate employee compensation, notably the service sector. Fourth, the absolute quality of the labour force grew in response to improved facilities for acquiring education and industrial skills, and perhaps increased more rapidly than the quality of capital.

However, these influences take effect gradually, and their impact upon income distribution is difficult to reconcile with the concentration into three periods of the rise in labour's income: from 55.3 per cent to 67.4 per cent of G.N.P. between 1910–14 and 1921–4, from a lower 67.1 per cent to 73.0 per cent between 1935–8 and 1946–9, and from 73.6 per cent to 80.2 per cent between 1964–8 and 1975. Owen Smith suggested that a fifth contributory cause of the increase in labour's share might be the growth of trade unions over the last hundred years. The union impact on income distribution may of course vary in strength at different times within a given institutional framework, while their actions can modify or alter that framework.

Baran and Sweezy (1966) argued that income distribution is determined by a complex of influences in which the actions of employers are more important than those of trade unions. Unions protect their members from insecurities that threaten the unorganised but they find it difficult to eat into profits since firms can pass on higher labour costs in increased prices and so maintain profit margins. They are also able to adjust their production methods, the quality of their product and the size of their labour force to safeguard profits. In the United Kingdom around half the occupied population do not belong to a trade union, while some are members of weak organisations, so that any union wage effect may be diluted over the whole economy. For these reasons unions often fail to increase real wages when they push up money wages, and merely initiate or fuel an inflationary spiral. The impact of their activities may be to achieve a redistribution within labour's share.

If trade unions prove successful in redistributing a part of profit margins, they face the problem of diverting capitalist consumption expenditure to their members without impairing investment. Unions can only achieve a permanent redistribution of a growing national income when their actions induce a rise in the capitalist propensity to consume. Conversely this propensity might fall, and the profit share increase, during a period of union weakness. However, a minimum rate of return on capital exists below which investment declines, while any increase in the property share tends to stimulate investment until continued accumulation depresses profits once more. Workers forgo income in a capitalist economy not only to provide the profits and interest required for inducing the owners of property to part with their liquidity but also to finance the consumption standards they develop. The essential prerequisite for trade unions to achieve their aim of raising labour's share to the maximum consistent with the maintenance of the long-run wage level is the socialisation of investment funds and the corresponding public ownership of the means of production.

Have trade unions contributed to upward displacements of labour's share within the existing institutional framework? A survey of the international evidence yields only tentative conclusions. Kuznets (1955) concluded that the E.C. share was positively correlated with the level of real income per head. As unions tend to obtain greater coverage in the richest countries, it is tempting to argue that their activities are responsible for such a correlation. Robinson and Eatwell (1973) claimed that the size of labour's share varies between countries according to the strength and militancy of unions. However, other influences may produce the observed relationship; for instance, the proportion of the occupied population that is self-employed tends to vary inversely with *per capita* income and may be responsible for the association between the E.C. share and real income per head. The research of Loftus (1969) confirms this suspicion, since it uncovered only minimal variations in the E.C. share within the manufacturing sector between rich and poor countries.

The upward trend of labour's share within many individual countries may be related to greater union strength, but confident assertions are difficult to make. Trade unions were too small to affect national distributive trends in the United States before the 1930s; in the latter decade a growth of unionisation accompanied an E.C. increase, but the effects of a severe depression and of the New Deal legislation were other possible causes of this distributive change. Jeck (1968) found that the labour share fell in Germany during the period of Nazi rule, but it is uncertain how far this was due to the destruction of the union movement and how far to the cyclical upswing in profits during the trade recovery.

Phelps Brown (1957a) argued from U.K. experience that relative union strength is an inadequate single explanation of distributive changes. To explain shifts between labour and property income he stressed the interaction of two forces: trade-union power and the market environment. The level of union power varies over time and is reflected in an upward pressure upon money wages of differing intensity; where unions are strong they can increase money wages rapidly, but where they are weak they lack this ability. The nature of the market environment is defined by the response of firms to changes in costs. When cost increases can be passed on to the consumer in higher prices, the market is 'soft'; when greater costs must be absorbed because competition prevents an increase in product prices, the market is 'hard'. In a soft market a rise in the money income of one class need not cause a change in distribution, because prices can be raised subsequently and all money incomes can increase by the same amount. Money wages and prices rise together and an inflationary spiral results, but distributive shares remain unaltered. In hard markets the scope for increasing prices is restricted, so that a rise in the money income secured by one group reduces the share of other groups. If trade unions can raise the cost to employers of disagreeing with their claims, they may prove able to redistribute income in favour of their members in a hard market by pushing up money wages and so squeezing profits.

Phelps Brown's (1957a) argument implies that no redistribution between labour and property incomes occurs in soft markets with strong unions or in hard markets with weak unions. There will be a shift towards labour when markets are hard and unions strong, and a shift towards property when weak unions face a soft market environment. Thus trade unions advanced money wages between 1909 and 1914, yet the E.C. share fell slightly as most firms passed on higher costs to consumers. Conversely the E.C. share rose a little in the late 1870s and early 1880s (despite the collapse of a number of unions under the impact of adverse trade conditions) because the prevailing hard market prevented capitalists from raising prices to redistribute income in favour of profits.

Phelps Brown (1957a) claimed that property incomes enjoyed relative gains when unions were weak and markets were soft. The wage share fell by 3.2 per cent between 1903 and 1906 at a time of rising prices when union activity was inhibited by the Taff Vale judgement of 1901.[7] The years between 1926 and 1928 saw a rapid recovery from the dislocation of the First World War and the postwar depression, the index of national income at 1900 price levels rising from 101.6 (1926) to 111.8 (1928). Unions were unable to secure an equivalent rise in their members' living standards because of their lack of bargaining power after their defeat in the General Strike of 1926, which led to a severe fall in their membership and financial reserves despite rising production and employment. Consequently the wage share fell by 2.2 per cent in these years.

On this line of reasoning we would anticipate the three periods in the United Kingdom when labour's share rose markedly to be characterised by a strong trade-union movement and a hard market environment. The labour share of gross national product rose by 12.1 per cent between 1910–14 and 1921–4, when on any definition union power increased. This distributive movement was substantial and proved permanent despite the cyclical fluctuations of the interwar years. During the war a large stimulus to demand caused a general expansion of prices and incomes, but a sharp deflation followed immediately. Falling prices and profits led to pressure for wage cuts, but a union movement with more than double its pre-war membership resisted and from 1919 to 1921 there was an unprecedented number of industrial disputes and working days lost. The attempts by unions to prevent money-wage reductions were defeated in many instances, but the effect of their resistance was to delay these reduc-

tions and often to diminish them. Consequently prices fell more
rapidly than money wages. The share of profits was squeezed by a
combination of deflationary markets and trade-union endeavours to
maintain the level of money wages. Other influences operated in the
same direction in this period. There was a fall in the proportion of
income generated by agriculture, where the labour share was low,
and a rise in the proportion generated by public service, where the
share was high. The numerical importance of self-employment
declined and skilled employment expanded, while the war-time inflation and the introduction of legislative controls reduced the share of
rent. Consequently the rise in labour's share during and immediately
after the First World War occurred in response to a number of
factors, of which the growth in union strength[8] would appear to have
been a necessary but not a sufficient condition. However, U.K.
experience cannot be generalised to other countries; in Sweden the
labour share did not increase at this time despite a rapid growth in the
membership and coverage of its trade unions.

The labour share of U.K. gross national product rose by 5.9 per
cent from 1935–8 to 1946–9 in response to an unusual combination
of circumstances. War mobilisation was accompanied by a continuously high demand for labour and the virtual elimination of
unemployment, which stood above 10 per cent of the insured workforce in each of the interwar years. Measures of rationing, price and
rent control and profit restraint were regarded as essential for achieving class co-operation in the war effort. These developments led to
wages rising faster than incomes derived from the ownership of
property (average wage incomes rose by 18 per cent between 1938
and 1947, while the average property income fell by 15 per cent).
Over the same period unionisation increased from 29.8 per cent to
44.4 per cent, and the power and prestige of the union movement
grew enormously in response to its detailed and wholehearted
involvement in the war effort. Indeed the T.U.C. became virtually a
department of the coalition government and inevitably claimed the
rights which flowed from such a responsibility. The Second World
War produced an inflationary climate, but the stringent price controls
operated to limit the degree to which cost increases could be passed
on to the consumer. Thus prices increased by only 6 per cent between
1942 and 1945. Moreover, the rapid increase in total money income
led to a fall in the real value of rents, which were subject to political
control and were frequently fixed in money terms for a long period in

advance. Again, the growth of union strength in this period appears to have been at least a permissive influence enabling the rise in labour's share to occur.

The profits squeeze in the United Kingdom during the last decade is likely to have some connection with increased union power, reflected by the growth in unionisation since 1967 after nineteen years of relative stagnation and by the greater number and length of industrial disputes in the late 1960s and early 1970s. Glyn and Sutcliffe (1972) advanced an explanation of recent distributive movements that closely resembles the model of Phelps Brown (1957a), in that property incomes were seen as being squeezed between progressively more severe international competition and an intensified wage push by trade unions. Despite accelerating inflation a given change in money wages produced an increasing impact on profits because of a harder international market environment in which a smaller percentage of cost increases could be passed on to consumers. Such a market environment arose from the expansion of world trade and the reduction of tariff levels, which led to countries becoming increasingly vulnerable to import penetration despite growing concentration of domestic industry. Rapid inflation tends to produce state action that restricts the growth of home demand, and so stimulates international competition as firms divert their sales activity abroad to absorb surplus capacity. Since 1940 full employment created a more militant working class with rising expectations, which in conjunction with intensified foreign competition threatens profitability. In these circumstances wage push can increase labour's share. Because falling property incomes lead to a decline in capital accumulation and employment, a greater labour share can be permanently safeguarded only by action to modify or replace the private ownership of capital.

However, the gradual growth of union power after thirty years' experience of full employment is not the sole cause of recent distributive changes, since the intensification of international competition was a crucial precipitating factor. The series in Tables 5.1 and 5.2 suggest that a tightening of the squeeze on property incomes took place after the wage explosion of 1969 and 1970, though this may have been partly caused by cyclical oscillations. The figures for 1976 indicate a reversal of the increase in labour's share, perhaps in response to government policies to safeguard profit margins. It is more difficult to believe that unions played a significant role in recent

U.S. income-distribution changes; for instance, the comprehensive explanation of Nordhaus (1974) does not rely in any way upon union bargaining power.

Phelps Brown's (1957a) theory and its subsequent development embody an important change in emphasis by providing trade unions with an explicit redistributive role. The existence of powerful unions is crucial for labour's resistance to attempts at raising the profit share, particularly when a fall in real wages is involved. Such a resistance often results in a prices–incomes spiral and helps to explain many of the wage disputes in recent years. However, while the weight of evidence suggests that trade unions possess some influence upon income distribution, it is too fragmentary, and the number of counter examples too large, to support the view that union bargaining power is the sole, or even the dominant, explanation of the pattern and course of relative shares. No U.K. study of income distribution has yet related changes in relative shares to an objective measure of some aspects of union strength, such as the degree and rate of change of unionisation. Some research has been conducted on these lines in the United States,[9] and despite the conceptual and statistical inadequacies of such measures comparable U.K. studies could prove a fruitful area for future investigation.

Historical experience is more complex than Phelps Brown (1957a) indicated, and his interpretation of the upward displacements of labour's share requires greater examination. However, it has the merit of stressing the importance of market imperfections and bargaining power to distributive changes. The distribution of income depends not only upon technical conditions of production but also upon the property relationships existing within the economy. Further advances in our understanding require the development of a theoretical structure in which the social environment within which price and income determination takes place is regarded as a variable rather than a constant parameter. In any such theory the bargaining power of trade unions becomes a central feature.

CONCLUSION

The lack of sizeable fluctuations in the wage share of U.K. national income since 1860 led many observers to claim that the proportion paid to labour has been constant. However, the distinction between jobs paid by wages and jobs paid by salaries has become less significant, and when the salary share is added to the wage share, labour's income rose relative to property income. This rise has been concentrated almost entirely into three periods: those around the two world wars, and that since 1968. The maximum possible labour share is the national income minus the funds required to maintain and improve the capital stock, while the minimum share is set by the subsistence wage. In a capitalist economy the upper limit is below the potential maximum due to consumption expenditure by capitalists.

On present evidence any assessment of the trade-union impact upon labour's share can only be tentative. From the complex of influences affecting income distribution union activity does not appear to have been decisive, though it was significant in the United Kingdom under certain conditions at certain times. Goodwin's (1967) account of the long-run development of capitalism stressed the limited scope available to unions for increasing labour's share. Such a conclusion may be modified in the future, if unionisation increases further and new strategies are pursued that draw upon new sources of power. When capital is state-owned it is necessary to withdraw funds from consumption to finance accumulation but the labour share can reach a higher maximum consistent with the long-run maintenance and growth of national income. In these circumstances a small minority of owners of capital need no longer control business activity, since the decision-making process could be extended democratically to trade unions and their members.

6

Trade Unions and the Process of Production

INTRODUCTION

INTRODUCTION

In Chapter 2 trade-union development was analysed in the context of employer-bargaining dominance in unorganised markets, which extends beyond wage negotiations to control of the process of production and of the activity of workers who participate in it. Once the contract of employment is completed workers become subject to a disciplinary structure designed to maximise the effort and application they supply in return for wages, so that the job environment and behaviour in the work-place are prescribed for them. Their inability to influence the decisions that immediately shape their lives may be more irksome than are the inequalities of income distribution. Unions attempt to obtain such influence by using collective-bargaining machinery to regulate the contents and conditions of their members' jobs.

THE RELATIONSHIP BETWEEN CAPITAL AND LABOUR

Modern industry can be organised under various types of relationship between the suppliers of capital and the suppliers of labour power:

(i) *Managerial autonomy*. This is the usual situation before the development of effective unions. Workers are treated solely as factors of production, are subject to a discipline imposed by employers and possess no collective-bargaining rights. All decisions are taken by the suppliers of capital or by managers they hire to act in their interests.

(ii) *Collective bargaining*. This represents the type of relationship that has evolved in Western mixed economies for most manual workers. Independent trade unions restrict employers' authority by bargaining over a range of issues, mainly pay and conditions of service. Union activity is predominantly defensive, since employers retain all organisational initiatives and thus determine the framework within which collective negotiations occur. Clegg (1951) argued that the effective opposition of unions to employers produces an industrial democracy, but the analogy is imperfect: political oppositions seek to form a government, but unions do not oppose with a view to securing control of companies.

(iii) *Participation*. This involves the consultation of workers during the process of industrial decision-making, as in the West German system of 'co-determination'. Workers are represented on boards of directors or other executive bodies and major employer initiatives are discussed with their representatives before being implemented.

(iv) *Workers' control*. This is the transitional stage of a strategy for augmenting the influence of workers. Building on existing shop-floor controls, the aim is to provide workers with an effective veto on employers' decisions and with sufficient bargaining power to impose their desired policy. This programme is often coupled with demands for extended public ownership.

(v) *Workers' self-management*. This is the ultimate evolution of workers' control in which executive powers are exercised by labour. Managers are elected, and subject to recall, by the workforce which determines the shop-floor environment. The conventional employer–worker distinction disappears and labour is no longer treated as a factor of production. Yugoslavia provides the only case of an economic system approximating to this model.

MANAGERIAL AUTONOMY

The contract of employment is distinguished from other contracts by at least two important peculiarities. First, the owner of labour power cannot be dissociated physically from the services it renders. Second, the conditions under which labour power is supplied vary greatly between a multiplicity of decentralised business establishments. Consequently the employers' implementation of the authority vested in them by the employment contract determines the job environment, and hence a crucial component of the standard of living, of their workforce. The employers' power derives from their ownership of property, the law of contract and their bargaining strength.

Employers and individual workers, although legally equal, are always unequal in practice. Under the terms of the contract the workman agrees to serve his employer, who is entitled to issue orders. Workers cannot alter the conditions of employment without employers' consent, but employers seeking change need only provide instructions that workers are expected to obey. The status of labour power as a commodity leads to a lack of power in its owners; by selling his labour power the worker is effectively transferring it for a stipulated period to the employer, who determines its development through his organisation of the methods of production.

In order to reap the benefits of factory organisation employers design a formal or informal code of discipline for their workforce which inevitably restricts certain areas of its freedom. A number of sanctions for this code can be devised, of which the most widespread has traditionally been fear of dismissal. In the 'scientific management' approach the method of wage payment, through some form of piece rate or bonus incentive, regulates the effort supplied, while the 'human relations' school stresses the importance of better shop-floor relationships for improving a labour force's productive potential. Whatever sanctions are used individual workers can exercise little direct control over their job environment or the pattern of behaviour expected of them.

Moreover, workers tend to view employers as the source of workshop disorder through their initiation of changes in production methods. In a dynamic economy the number and character of jobs available is continually subject to alterations in techniques and market demands, so that no firm is able to offer more than a limited security to its labour force. Individual workers cannot influence the scale and pace of innovation, though the latter may increase the hazards of work, reduce the number of men employed, alter the character of skills required and/or divide productive tasks into a series of consecutive operations. Such division often causes boredom, nervous strain and a lower sense of achievement.

The lack of fulfilment offered by many contemporary jobs has created renewed interest in theories of alienation. Fromm (1965) argued that the most important cause of alienation lay in the individual worker's lack of control over the conditions, the instruments and the products of his labour, so that his need for creativity and self-respect remains unsatisfied.[1] Workers seek to overcome this lack of control by establishing a framework of rights to protect themselves from unilateral employer decisions; the need for such protection stimulated trade-union development. Unions attempt to shape the conditions under which their members work through collective bargaining, and some writers, for example Fox (1971), believe that union limitations upon the use of labour after its hire have more significant implications than their impact on wages.

COLLECTIVE BARGAINING

Informal rules to achieve a partial control over the job environment have existed among work-groups since the beginning of industrial production. One of the earliest formal attempts to regulate the management of labour was made by craft unions in the nineteenth century, based on their ability to control the entry of skilled workers into their trade. In many firms craft control developed through the establishment of 'custom and practice' into a more sophisticated constraint on the employers' freedom to determine the organisation of work, recruitment, discipline and technical change. The growth of union membership among unskilled workers, particularly during two world wars, created a wider base for effective collective negotiations, which in many industries replaced employer authority with joint regulation. After 1940 full employment permitted the extension of work-place bargaining, with shop stewards negotiating over a range of issues through their regular opportunities to revise piecework payments. In recent years the scale and importance of initiatives at shop-floor level have increased with the pace of modern technological innovation and the complexity of administering large organisations. Thus collective bargaining enables employees not only to secure higher living standards but to share decision-making on certain industrial issues vital to them. Unions reduce the power exercised by employers, whose dominance is modified by an accumulating body of industrial jurisprudence, so that agreed procedures must be undertaken before substantial changes are made in the value or character of existing jobs.

Living standards are influenced not only by wages but also by certain non-pecuniary terms of employment, each of which contributes to a trade union's overall welfare goal:

(i) Unions seek security of job tenure for their members and the formal or informal acceptance of arrangements for the incidence of redundancy and work-sharing should unemployment prove inevitable; thus a frequent demand is that lay-offs occur in reverse order of seniority. In essence unions assert that their members' right to a job is a species of property rights.

(ii) Unions influence hours of work and the number of days of holiday with pay. Over a long period the standard working week has grown shorter, thereby reducing the ratio of hours paid at the basic rate to the total number worked. Individual unions vary in their attitudes to overtime, some attempting to maximise overtime hours as a temporary expedient.

(iii) Unions try to persuade both employers and the state to improve working conditions. During the 1960s the number of factory accidents rose from 150,000 to over 300,000 per annum and the working days lost as a result were between four and five times higher than those lost through disputes. Therefore, issues of industrial health, such as the disposal of machinery, methods of operation and the provision of safety equipment, are of central concern to workers.

(iv) While attempting to raise earnings levels unions also influence the method of wage payment. Preferences differ between industries and occupations, though there is a current shift of opinion towards time-rate and away from piece-rate systems.

(v) Unions endeavour to provide their members with an increasing measure of control over their job environment, procedures for initiating changes and the machinery for implementing industrial discipline.

Wilkinson and Burkitt (1973) argued that a trade union's economic objective could be summarised as an attempt to secure at any point in time an optimum combination of the various components of its members' living standards.

This objective is pursued through collective bargaining, which can be defined as an arrangement for settling wages and working conditions by agreement between an employer, or an association of employers, and an association of employees. Such arrangements are practicable only when workers are represented by a trade union which has obtained the right to negotiate on their behalf, a provision that causes strife until employers grant recognition to unions. It is also necessary for some recognised negotiating procedure to be established. Collective bargaining is an important institution in all industrialised countries which allow freedom of association, but it varies in detail between different countries, between different industries in the same country, and of course it evolves through time. Collective agreements contain the currently negotiated wages and conditions, together with specification of the procedure to be followed should a dispute occur. Bargaining involves not merely reaching agreement on terms but extends to their subsequent administration and interpretation, though both parties usually reserve the right to coerce the other through the imposition of sanctions that inflict costs of disagreement.

MacIver and Page (1953) saw bargaining as 'the process by which the antithetical interests of supply and demand, of buyer and seller, are adjusted to end in an act of exchange'. This description fits individual bargains where work is exchanged for wages but collective bargaining possesses additional characteristics. It is not an act of exchange but rather a rule-making process designed to regulate the terms contained in employment contracts. Trade unions do not sell labour, nor do employers' associations buy it, but their agreements impose limits on their members' freedom by formulating rules which prevent favouritism and arbitrary discrimination. Responsibility for the content and enforcement of these rules is shared by the employers' associations and unions which jointly determine them.

Chamberlain (1951) argued that collective bargaining fulfils three functions. It is a means of contracting for the sale of labour, a form of industrial government and a method of management. To some extent the exercise of these functions is chronological. When recognised by employers, unions first negotiate to fix terms for the sale of labour, then provisions are required for the settlement of disputes and finally collective agreements seek to regulate the use of labour after its hire. Slichter, Healy and Livernash (1960) identified three methods by which unions limit employers' authority:

(i) by requiring that employers follow agreed rules on issues affecting their members, such as lay-offs, promotion, retirement, overtime assignment, production standards and work speeds;

(ii) by requiring that employer actions on matters for which no relevant rules exist are 'fair', 'reasonable', 'with just cause' or occur after consultation or with the consent of the union;

(iii) by prohibiting certain types of conduct.

Flanders (1970) argued that union negotiation of employment contracts protects members' material standards of living, while regulation of labour management protects their security, status and self-respect.

The managerial and government functions of collective bargaining possess significant social implications because they create a code of industrial rights which to some degree protects workers from market fluctuations, technical change and employer decisions. The character of wage negotiations alters when their scope is extended, since the weight of argument moves from the economic to the social and ethical.[2] Rehn (1957) considered unions to be part of 'the revolt against the market' because they create a secondary system of industrial citizenship supplementary to the system of political citizenship. Therefore, an enduring achievement of trade unionism is the creation of a social order in industry embodied in a code of workers' rights, and protection of these rights is a service offered continuously to members.

An example of this aspect of union activity is the recent (1978) negotiations in the U.K. engineering industry for revision of the 1922 York Memorandum, which requires workers to operate any changed methods and accept any managerial decisions until their grievances are put through the recognised procedure, which can take several months to complete. The unions now demand that, pending agreement, no change may be implemented if it leads to workers' objections, so that the status quo would apply during negotiations. If this demand were conceded, workers would possess a veto over a wide range of employer decisions. Such a development would supplement the increased bargaining activity of shop stewards in the work-place that has developed since 1940 under conditions of full employment.

However, the rights of industrial citizenship gained by trade unions for their members remain limited. The union role within collective bargaining is essentially defensive, for much of their activity involves reacting to the policies of those possessing command over finance and other productive resources. The environment within which union participation in the regulation of wages and working conditions occurs is determined by previous interlocking employers' decisions, for instance on the scale of production, the location of industry, investment, technology, manning levels, safety and welfare. Unions encroach on these decisions only to a limited degree and the controls achieved over such phenomena as manning and the speed of the production line were not conceded readily; McCarthy (1966) found that most managements still regard agreement to recognise unions as a substantial concession on their part. Moreover, collective agreements are in practice implemented by managerial representatives of the employer. The need for business flexibility, when interpreting general rules, creates the personal and continuous character of authority in firms.

A shifting frontier of control divides workers' rights from the employer's prerogatives and its exact location is determined by the distribution of power within an enterprise. Between 1940 and 1970 U.K. unions enjoyed thirty years of full employment during which they achieved a substantial measure of job regulation in certain industries (e.g. engineering and printing), but employers still exercise largely unfettered control over many crucial decisions. They draw up corporate financial accounts, which unions have no independent means of checking, and their decisions determine the conditions under which unions negotiate. By contrast unions possess little influence in most areas of industrial decision-making. The strike is their most powerful weapon for imposing costs upon employers, but it is unwieldy to use and vulnerable to counter-pressure from capital, the state and the communications media. An essential requirement for more effective union participation in collective bargaining is a flow of regular data on the relevant firms' manpower, earnings and finance, and sections 17 to 21 of the Employment Protection Act of 1975 placed a duty on employers to disclose the information required for collective bargaining to union negotiators.

Therefore, trade unions place important constraints of consultation, and sometimes prohibition, upon the autonomy of employers. Arbitrary rule has been increasingly replaced in certain industries by jointly agreed rules ensuring consistency of treatment. However, the basic policy decisions in industry are still determined by the financial interests of employers, who largely structure the pattern of relationships within their enterprises. Collective bargaining restricts their authority, but to date the industrial power structure has yielded little to union activity, which takes place against a background of continuing inequality reflected in lifetime earnings, conditions of work, the intrinsic character of jobs and the experience of power relationships.

PARTICIPATION

The West German practice of participation is normally termed 'co-determination'. Under the Works Constitution Law, firms outside coal-mining and steel are overseen by a supervisory board, charged to uphold the shareholders' interests, but one-third of which is composed of elected worker representatives. This structure of participation provides an increased flow of information to individual workers and gives them a greater opportunity to express suggestions and grievances through their representatives. However, minority representation fails to transform the unions' basically defensive role, since it does not extend joint regulation to industrial policy-making nor enables workers to play an active role in shaping their job environment. Therefore, subjective opinions as to the desirability of an extension of workers' control condition reactions to co-determination. Those who wish to maintain the existing industrial order but with a greater consultation of the labour force see co-determination as a beneficial advance in industrial democracy, but those who desire a fundamental shift in the balance of power towards workers believe it to be a means of incorporating labour within the authority structures designed by capital.

In coal and steel, representation on the supervisory board is on a fifty–fifty basis and recent legislative proposals seek to extend this formula to all enterprises with more than 2000 employees. These proposals have aroused great controversy; they would extend workers' influence, but to a limited extent, since they stipulate that the board's chairman should always be a shareholders' nominee and that one worker representative must be elected by the managerial staff. The significance of such reforms depends upon the authority exercised by supervisory boards. Davies (1975) concluded that 'it is on a board with essentially limited powers, certainly with powers that fall far short of an effective voice in collective bargaining, that the employees are represented in Germany'. It would therefore seem that co-determination provides institutional machinery permitting a greater consultation of workers within individual enterprises but does not in itself transform the structure of industrial power.

WORKERS' CONTROL AND WORKERS' SELF-MANAGEMENT

Coates and Topham (1972) distinguished 'self-management' where executive powers in an enterprise are exercised by workers, from 'control' – the transitional situation through which self-management is to be attained. This distinction is crucial to any analysis of the process by which changes in the capital–labour relationship are achieved, but for our purposes the two situations can be discussed jointly as ones in which workers possess an effective veto on industrial decisions and so structure their shop-floor environment by determining the tasks to be performed, the conditions under which they are carried out and the compensation offered in return. Any development in this direction would reverse past trends towards the separation of managerial and non-managerial tasks by eliminating the distinction between employers and workers.

Proposals for some form of workers' control possess a long history[3] and formed the basis of the guild socialists' programme,[4] but they became more insistent during the last decade as part of the reaction against large, impersonal organisations and in response to the desire of many workers for greater control over their lives. This movement of opinion was reflected in the proposals of the Bullock Report for worker directors and given impetus by the establishment of a number of experimental workers' co-operatives with government financial support (e.g. the Meriden motor-cycle factory and the *Scottish Daily News* venture). Demands for the extension of workers' control originate from shop-floor pressure that restrains the exercise of employers' authority, and the method of achieving these demands is usually envisaged as the extension of collective bargaining from a partial regulation of the immediate job environment to cover all items of concern to the workforce. Such an extension would enforce a greater measure of accountability upon industrial decision-making.

In response to the increased interest in proposals for workers' control, a number of economists have developed theoretical models of self-management. These conclude that an economy of labour-managed enterprises operating under the same technical conditions and the same requirements of free entry and exit as the traditional entrepreneurial economy would be equally capable of attaining the 'Pareto-optimal' allocation of resources.[5] Advocates of self-management, such as Vanek (1970), claim that this conclusion supports their case. However, if imperfect competition prevails, self-managed enterprises may restrict production to maximise earnings per current worker. Conflict can also arise on the issues of charging for external costs and benefits, the rate of investment and the control of inflation. Shackleton (1976) argued that such conflicts can only be resolved by the existence of a state administration acting as a centralised co ordinating agency to especially prevent labour-managed enterprises in a not very competitive economy from initiating inflation by raising their incomes through price increases. Theoretical models of self-management indicate that the system does not solve the complex problems faced by industrial economies in itself, but they have not established that it is inherently less efficient than the capitalist or centrally planned alternatives on conventional economic criteria. It may also yield social gains, such as an enhancement of workers' dignity or a reduction in discontent.

Yugoslavia possesses the only economy currently using self-management on a large scale. Its use did not develop through the application of an ideological blueprint, but as a practical means of economic development in a country with strong internal antagonisms and hostility to central control. No industrial enterprises are based on the private ownership of capital and the self-managed unit is an independent trading agency. There is little central direction of production, so that these units operate in a largely market economy. They obtain capital through self-financing and borrowing from public agencies, on which interest is paid. Depreciation is set aside from current income to preserve assets and the use of accumulated internal finance is at the enterprise's discretion. Managers are responsible to a works council, which appoints the director of the enterprise for a four-year term and establishes its administrative structure. The works council determines income distribution, the level of reserves and the method of capital funding.

The Yugoslav economy has been characterised by the determination of enterprises to maintain output and employment despite national economic vicissitudes. Capital accumulation is encouraged by the high level of depreciation funds available for reinvestment, the tax advantages of investing out of income, the favourable terms for loans and the variety of sources of finance. Theoretical models of self-management suggest that two difficulties may be a restriction of output to maintain income and a favouring of consumption at the expense of investment. Yugoslavia's experience shows that these pitfalls can be avoided. Industrial production has grown very rapidly at a rate between 5 and 15 per cent per annum. However, the rate of inflation has been among the greatest in the world outside South America. In practice the control of inflation has proved the most intractable problem facing a self-managed economy.

An extension of workers' control requires the existence of established channels of communication between workers and their representatives; trade-union organisation is the most obvious of such channels, though its use in this way would be dependent upon improved standards of accountability. The desirability of a shift in power towards workers, to the extent that they can veto decisions affecting the process of production, is highly controversial. The supporters of such a change stress that it could lead to increased productive efficiency, since the greater security enjoyed by workers will create a less defensive attitude, thus enabling a more rapid rate of innovation. A wider range of abilities may be tapped and effort intensified, for there is considerable evidence suggesting that job satisfaction rises with the level of involvement in work.[6] To be effective decision-making depends ultimately upon the consent of those affected, and many argue that industry will become increasingly difficult to organise without a substantial extension of workers' influence. However, advocates of self-management emphasise its democratic justification on the basis of political analogies and of the 'property rights' workers acquire in jobs through their investment of effort, skill and time; thus they tend to regard any gains in efficiency as a beneficial side-effect.

In contrast opponents of changes in the structure of industrial authority stress the importance of private property rights for the maintenance of individual liberty based on a decentralisation of power. They also argue that productive efficiency would be damaged if the profit incentive is lost and that labour-managed enterprises will be concerned to preserve jobs rather than to seek new trading opportunities. Moreover, management's prerogatives may be essential for the exercise of the technical expertise it alone possesses and for securing access to specialised skills and a flow of finance. Consequently opposition to self-management is based on the threats to political freedoms and economic efficiency that it is believed to pose. Since self-management proposals are designed essentially to transfer power from capital to labour, opinions about them largely depend upon subjective judgements as to the 'best' distribution of power in an economy. The controversy becomes even more intractable when extensions of workers' control are linked to public ownership; indeed, Coates and Topham (1972) argued that nationalisation is a necessary but not a sufficient condition for self-management.[7]

THE POLITICAL ROLE OF UNIONS

Trade-union attempts to control their members' job environment inevitably extend beyond the work-place. In mixed economies unions engage in political activity to affect the social and institutional conditions that influence their performance in collective bargaining. Due to their lack of finance and their normally weak bargaining position, individual workers exert a smaller impact on the formulation and operation of government policy than do employers, and unions seek to counter the political power based on ownership of capital by lobbying as a pressure group on behalf of the labour force, either in one sector or nationally. A collective policy possesses greater authority than individual opinions, which often require group activity to be articulated. Union political activities are both specific and general; they advocate particular items of legislation to further members' interests, but they also campaign for wider social reforms. They tend to associate with a political party, though the character of the association varies from the informal, as in the United States, to the institutional links between unions and socialist parties in the United Kingdom and Scandinavia. The precise nature of their political role varies according to the prevailing relationship between capital and labour.

Interest groups do not compete on equal terms for political influence. Trade-union power is exercised in a more overt way, through strike activity, than the power of other groups, and it increased between 1940 and 1970 under the impact first of war-time consultations and then the maintenance of full employment. There is a wide measure of agreement that unions enable a more effective representation of workers' interests, but there is considerable controversy as to whether unions can accumulate greater political strength than employers. Many believe that unions have now established sufficient power through the increased impact of strike activity to impose their desired policies upon governments. Others, including the present authors, argue that capitalists still enjoy a dominant position in the power structure confronting the state because of the control of resources which their ownership inevitably entails. Judgement on where the balance of power lies depends upon political philosophy and the interpretation of current events. Detailed arguments on each side were put forward by Brittan (1976) and Burkitt (1977), and opinions as to whether union political power is excessive or deficient will exert considerable influence upon future political and economic debate. The relationship between trade unions and the state operates in two directions: union political activity is designed to obtain desired government action; yet through both specific legislation and the development of general policies governments affect the practices and achievements of unions. The latter topic is considered in Chapter 7.

CONCLUSION

Any assessment of the overall effects of trade unions must be based on their social and political, as well as economic, consequences. Unions attempt to improve their members' non-pecuniary conditions of work in addition to raising their earnings. Workers become subject to a continuous and flexible discipline after agreeing terms of employment and unions seek to contain, and if possible to regulate jointly, the impact of this discipline upon their members.

In an industrial economy the relationship between the suppliers of capital and the suppliers of labour power can take a variety of forms. Where unions fail to develop effective bargaining strength the relationship is one of managerial autonomy, where employers, or their hired administrators, possess almost complete freedom to determine the organisation of production. For most manual workers in Western mixed economies the employers' ability to determine their job environment is restricted in varying degrees by trade unions through formal collective negotiations and informal shop-floor procedures. The countervailing power of unions, particularly at workshop level, has increased substantially since 1940 in such industries as engineering and printing, but it still remains a largely defensive reaction, amounting at most to the ability to obstruct the decisions of others.

The authority of employers to reach decisions unilaterally is being challenged by the spread of education among workers, by outright rejection of certain employer sanctions such as arbitrary dismissal and by the difficulty of administering large organisations. Consequently increased interest has been taken over the last decade in proposals to achieve greater workers' participation in industry, ranging from the development of consultation procedures to the formulation of blueprints for a system of self-management. Extension of union control on these lines would be consistent with the gradual widening of the areas covered by collective bargaining in the present century, but proposals that advance beyond improved consultation inevitably transfer power from capital to labour. The practicality of such proposals depends upon the existence of a sufficiently strong political will, and their desirability upon judgements about the kind of society towards which we should evolve – this latter question is too wide in scope to be discussed in this book. Whatever individual opinions on this issue our discussion suggests that a complete analysis of labour-market operations must begin with an examination of the social and political background from which suppliers of capital and labour start to bargain. In such analysis the character of bargaining activity becomes a variable in the process that determines wages and conditions of employment.

7

Trade Unions and the State

INTRODUCTION

The discussion in previous chapters demonstrated that the outcome of labour-market transactions possesses profound ramifications for social development. Consequently all governments are compelled to establish an industrial-relations policy, if only implicitly. This book is not designed to provide a comprehensive account of trade-union law, but no study of the unions' economic role would be complete without consideration of their relationship to the state. The traditional U.K. view has been that governments should not intervene in labour markets but should encourage employers and unions to participate in voluntary collective bargaining by providing laws which enable such a system to operate. Over the last decade a variety of developments combined to weaken this approach and produce a more active government role.

THE TRADITIONAL ROLE OF THE STATE IN THE UNITED KINGDOM

The Doctrine of Collective Laissez-Faire

Until the 1960s the predominant function of the state was to maintain voluntary collective bargaining and to secure the peaceful resolution of disputes between capital and labour through the conciliation procedures set up by the Ministry of Labour. This framework was based on the doctrine of collective *laissez-faire*, which held that the use of the law in labour markets should be reduced to a minimum, with employers and unions being encouraged to develop their own non-legal machinery. Only when such machinery breaks down should the government intervene to determine rules of conflict between the bargainers.

The support for voluntary bargaining among U.K. trade unions grew up during the nineteenth century, when certain unions attained considerable bargaining strength, yet their members had not secured the franchise. In these circumstances distrust of state intervention was widespread. For U.K. unions the essence of voluntarism is their right to self-government and their belief that law courts decide labour issues in a manner and on criteria alien to union traditions. This belief developed in response to their struggles against the courts' restrictions upon their ability to defend their members and will be modified only by experience of legislation favourable to them.[1] Preference for a voluntary settlement of industrial disputes is shared by most employers, as shown by their reluctance to invoke the provisions of the 1971 Industrial Relations Act designed to operate in their favour.

The Law and Industrial Relations

Acceptance of collective *laissez-faire* did not preclude the establishment of a legal framework for industrial relations. During the late eighteenth century pre-existing state intervention in the labour market fell into decay, but under the impact of the French Revolution and the Napoleonic wars hostility to trade unions was expressed through the Combination Acts of 1799 and 1800. After their repeal in 1825 governments adopted the equivocal position of tolerating union development while doing little to prevent its harassment by the courts. Between 1871 and 1913 a series of Acts of Parliament attempted to remove the obstacles to union activity created by judicial interpretations of common law. These Acts did not establish union rights but rather immunity from the penalties that would otherwise have followed collective action. For example, the central provision of the 1906 Trade Disputes Act, until recently the cornerstone of labour legislation, attempted to remove workers engaged in the prosecution of a dispute from liability for actions of civil conspiracy. U.K. laws provided no legal guarantee of the right to organise a strike, but removed such organisation from the threat of court proceedings, except for certain temporary restrictions as in the two world wars.

In the United States and most of Europe the law positively encourages collective bargaining; for instance, the 1935 National Labour Relations Act conferred on U.S. employees freedom to bargain collectively, while in France and Italy a written constitutional right to strike exists. The corollary is that collective agreements can be enforced as legal contracts, whose breach can lead to orders for damages or injunctions, so that a 'no-strike, no-lockout' obligation is imposed on unions and employers for the duration of the agreement. In practice this obligation favours employers, who can alter working conditions unilaterally. In contrast changes desired by workers can be imposed only through the threat of sanctions. The intention of U.K. employers and unions that their agreements should stand outside the law is a rare phenomenon, which is linked to the role of legislation in fostering union development by providing legal immunity from civil actions rather than positive encouragement.

Specific Government Interventions

U.K. acceptance of the doctrine of collective *laissez-faire* was compatible with the emergence of a positive state role, designed largely to support or supplement voluntary bargaining, in certain limited spheres:

(i) Governments have intervened to facilitate the settlement of industrial disputes, since the 1896 Conciliation Act offered employers and unions services of conciliation and arbitration in the event of disagreement.[2] The 1919 Industrial Courts Act imposed on the Ministry of Labour a duty to promote industrial harmony, traditionally interpreted as providing maximum inducement to reach agreement by voluntary negotiation rather than prescribing and enforcing specific terms. The Act also established the Industrial Court as a permanent arbitration body, though its awards are not legally binding. In the United Kingdom no final source for resolving disputes exists and state machinery for their settlement remains a complement, not an alternative, to collective bargaining.

(ii) The first effective Factory Act in 1833 established a precedent for state action to protect employees in a weak bargaining position. In 1909 the principle was extended by the formation of trade boards which fixed a legal minimum wage for workers in four 'sweated' industries through negotiations between the appropriate employers' and workers' organisations. The 1959 Wages Councils Act provides state-supported collective bargaining in industries not covered by

voluntary agreements and in 1978 around sixty wages councils perform this function, the post-1945 creations being mainly in the retail
trades. The state also provides a certain amount of more general
protection. The Factory Acts set minimum standards of health, safety
and welfare applicable to all employees, while the Terms and Conditions of Employment Act of 1959 established a statutory procedure
for compelling an employer to observe terms as favourable as those
determined collectively for his industry. This direct legislative provision supporting voluntary bargaining is enacted only on union
request in specific circumstances.

(iii) The award of public contracts to the lowest bidder creates
injustice if the bid is based upon low wages. To prevent this the 1946
Fair Wages Resolution stipulates that government departments
should require acceptable employment standards, including a fair-
wages clause, of their suppliers. By fair is meant 'wages . . . hours and
conditions of labour, not less favourable than those established' in the
relevant collective agreement, so that the state extends the application of union standards. The Resolution possesses no legal force but
nationalised industries and many local authorities include fair-wages
clauses in their contracts. Section 4 of the Fair Wages Resolution
states that 'the contractor shall recognise the freedom of his workpeople to be members of trade unions'; thus employers hostile to
unionism are unlikely to obtain government contracts.

(iv) The state's concern to protect private property and trade
during industrial disputes leads to control of various aspects of strike
activity, notably picketing. The formation of police 'strike flying
squads' and several court decisions curtailing the possibility of legal
picketing[3] led to increasing state regulation during the acceleration of
industrial conflict in the late 1960s and the early 1970s.

(v) Governments define the circumstances in which a strike
creates a state of 'emergency' and appropriate special powers to meet
such a contingency. The 1920 Emergency Powers Act of the United
Kingdom defined an 'emergency' as 'events of such a nature as to be
calculated . . . to deprive the community . . . of the essentials of life'.
The 1971 Industrial Relations Act added a wider dimension: 'an
interruption in the supply of goods or in the provision of services of
such a nature, or on such a scale, as to be likely to be gravely injurious
to the national economy'. This wider definition incorporated disputes
that might affect the balance of payments or the rate of inflation, thus
providing the state with extended discretionary powers.

THE CONTEMPORARY DEBATE

The philosophy of collective *laissez-faire* has come under severe attack during the last decade, with the result that relations between governments and trade unions have taken on a novel character. The most striking indication of this change has been a growing tendency for state intervention in matters previously regarded as the concern of employers and unions. This tendency developed in response to the government's increasing importance as an employer, union political activity, the international weakness of the U.K. economy, the search for an effective counter-inflation policy and a desire to minimise the frequency of industrial disputes.

The expansion of the public sector inevitably involved government directly in the determination of pay levels and thus undermined its role as a non-interventionist encourager of voluntary collective bargaining. 'Fair treatment' for state employees is usually defined as comparability with the current income of broadly equivalent private workers. The government's dilemma is to maintain such parity without becoming a pace-setter for increases in money incomes, an ever-present possibility when around a quarter of all employees work in the public sector. Consequently a state view of the desirable size of pay rises becomes unavoidable.

Trade-union political activity has mobilised opinion in support of government measures to provide safeguards against redundancy that involve a departure from collective *laissez-faire*. The 1963 Contracts of Employment Act established minimum periods of notice for workers, so restricting the scope for unilateral employer actions, while the Redundancy Payments Act of 1965 subsequently imposed the obligation upon firms to pay compensation to workers becoming redundant after two years of continuous employment.

Shonfield (1969) attacked the theoretical basis of collective *laissez-faire*; he argued that governments should pursue positive labour-market policies believing that they cannot be left solely to the parties directly involved but require a specific institutional framework supported by legislation. He wanted the law altered so that legally enforceable contracts between employers and unions became the normal practice. He argued that this change would accelerate industrial regeneration, because capitalists would invest more heavily and rapidly if they possessed the support of unions carrying out freely undertaken contractual obligations. The business climate would become more stable and stimulate innovation. Such proposals seek to base trade-union law on more interventionist principles than those of collective *laissez-faire* without directly curbing the exercise of union power. In a similar vein Kahn-Freund (1969) advocated legislation to remove the tension between Parliament and the law courts by stating precisely when and how the courts could intervene in industrial disputes.

However, the major impetus for the more active labour-market policies of successive governments over the last decade arose from their responsibility for the overall management of the economy. Growing awareness of the unsatisfactory relative performance of the U.K. economy, and in particular the acceleration of inflation, led the state to move from its traditional role of conciliator to more comprehensive intervention as pay regulator. Its industrial-relations and incomes policies directly challenged the results of collective bargaining. The specific problems posed for governments by cost-push inflation were the chief cause of this development.

THE POLICY PROBLEM OF COST-PUSH INFLATION

When inflation occurs as a result of excess demand, budgetary and monetary policies can, in principle, provide a cure. If, however, prices rise in response to cost-push forces, these tools of demand management are less effective. In Chapter 4 it was argued that modern inflation arises at least partly from changes in social and economic relationships produced by thirty years of full employment. In this environment reductions in demand over a wide range fail to induce a cut in money incomes; costs and prices fall only when deflationary policies are pursued vigorously over a considerable period. If aggregate demand is depressed to such an extent that inflationary cost mechanisms are broken, there is no guarantee, and perhaps little likelihood, that these mechanisms will not be re-established when demand revives. A permanently high level of unemployment, or recurrent slumps, may be necessary to contain inflation through budgetary or monetary policy, and these would depress investment and the rate of economic growth. Moreover, such a strategy is unlikely to win political acceptance. Before 1940 bankruptcy and unemployment were regarded as uncontrollable disasters, but today they are seen as a consequence of the government's policy and so cause its unpopularity. Therefore, reliance on budgetary and monetary policies is unlikely to steer the economy from cost inflation to steady growth and stable prices at full employment.

When governments concentrate upon the management of aggregate demand, politically acceptable levels of inflation and of unemployment may be incompatible under the labour-market conditions outlined in Chapter 4. Confronted by this dilemma state objectives alternate: a lack of jobs leads to expansionist measures, but rising prices and balance-of-payments difficulties subsequently produce deflationary fiscal and credit policies. If this cycle continues unchecked, it damages confidence, investment and growth. The short-run objective of governments is to break the momentum of inflation, while in the long run the rate of price increases must be continuously curbed without damage to employment prospects and living standards.

These objectives can only be achieved by alterations in the socio-economic environment and the attitudes it engenders. Governments possess a number of alternative strategies for directly restraining costs at each level of economic activity which modify the character of labour markets and the trade-union role within them. The increased ability of unions to raise money wages, and so contribute to cost-push inflation,[4] stimulates the need for new labour-market institutions and procedures. During the Second World War Kalecki (1943) argued that capitalism required a new social and political apparatus to accommodate the increased power of the working class at full employment. This adjustment appeared to have been accomplished successfully during the 1950s, but the experience of the last decade, when accelerating inflation was followed by unprecedentedly post-war unemployment, indicates that the issue remains open.

THE RESTRICTION OF TRADE-UNION BARGAINING POWER

One possible method of controlling cost-push inflation is to curtail by legislation the ability of trade unions to increase the level of money wages. Such a policy may be supplemented by the creation of unemployment. The theoretical case for legislation to curb union power is that it would enable markets to function competitively, reduce the strength of cost-push forces and ensure the conduct of industrial relations in a manner conducive to economic efficiency. Thus Hutt (1973) argued that union policies constitute monopolistic restraints of trade, whenever individuals are free to withdraw their labour and can refuse to work at the offered wage.

A variety of measures has been proposed to enact such a philosophy. Hutt (1973) advocated an 'Emancipation of Labour Bill' to 'rescue' the labour market from 'duress-imposed constraints'. A similar policy, suggested by Haberler (1972), involved a change of trade-union law, so that their leaders would be financially responsible for damages caused by breaches of contract, and the removal of 'subsidies' to strikers by altering the terms of income-tax rebates and social-security provision. Haberler argued that union bargaining weapons should be defined as restraints of trade under the existing restrictive practices legislation and those implementing them fined in the Restrictive Practices Court. These measures, in conjunction with a modification of minimum-wage legislation, would curb 'excess' union power.

Proposals of this type have created considerable controversy in the United Kingdom. After publication of the Labour Government's White Paper *In Place of Strife* debate centred on whether agreements between employers and unions on the procedures to be followed in disputes should be legally enforceable. The 1971 Industrial Relations Act attempted to regulate union bargaining strength by a series of anti-strike provisions,[5] financial penalties on the use of other union sanctions, and the registration and control of union rules. It was implemented by a new institution, the National Industrial Relations Court (N.I.R.C.).

The Act failed in its intended effects, since industrial conflict rose to new heights and it added official to unofficial militancy. It proved ineffective, partly because of the union counter-offensive[6] and partly because its ordinary provisions were invoked only on the initiative of individual employers. Large companies were reluctant to take such initiatives for fear of worsening future labour relations, so that controversy originated from cases precipitated by small firms or individual litigation.

The 1974 Labour Government replaced the Industrial Relations Act by the Trade Union and Labour Relations Act, which largely restored the pre-1971 legal position and was later supplemented by an Employment Protection Act designed to extend 'employees' rights and strengthen collective bargaining'. A new Conciliation and Arbitration service was also established. Thus attitudes to trade-union law recently passed through several marked phases in the

United Kingdom: the Donovan Commission (1969) advocated a mainly voluntarist approach, the 1971 Industrial Relations Act embodied the statutory philosophy, and since 1974 government intervention has been based largely upon the non-legal methods sanctioned by the social contract.

U.K. experience demonstrates the problems involved in legislative attempts to curb union bargaining power. The history of the Industrial Relations Act illustrated the ineffectiveness of laws considered 'unfair' by those to whom they apply. Thirty years of full employment enabled workers to escape from the constraints under which they previously sold their labour and they are unlikely to accept willingly laws re-establishing their bargaining weakness. Since 1945 inflation has been avoided through union weakness only under special circumstances; for example, between 1950 and 1955 in West Germany mass immigration and lack of finance created a pacific union policy.

The Industrial Relations Act also showed the reluctance of employers to enforce legal sanctions against their workers. The contravention of agreements could be made liable to criminal proceedings initiated by the state, but this method of enforcement did not reduce the incidence of unofficial strikes during the Second World War. The evidence collected by the Donovan Commission (1969) indicated the futility of legal sanctions for securing industrial peace; as most disputes last only a few days, the law would usually come into operation after the resumption of work and tend to re-open conflict.

Under the U.K. voluntary tradition collective bargaining evolved into a continuous process comprising a patchwork of formal agreements, informal understandings and 'custom and practice'. No court, asked to enforce a collective agreement, could separate it from the unwritten practices constituting its background, while legal sanctions would apply to uncertain norms – by general consent, an ineffective policy. Moreover, since 1945 the incidence of strikes in the United Kingdom has not been severe by international standards,[7] so that the possession of legally enforceable contracts does not necessarily reduce the working days lost through industrial disputes.

The practical problems of attempting a legal restriction of union power are reinforced by doubts about the relevance of its theoretical support. Hutt (1973) and Haberler (1972) failed to recognise that trade unions essentially counter the dominance of employers in unorganised markets, so that the effective application of their policies would weaken labour's position and change the power structure against those paid by earnings in favour of those owning property. Increased business competition and liberalisation of international trade, advocated by Haberler (1972), do not comprise an equivalent reduction in employers' strength, because in the absence of either monopolies or effective unions employers enjoy the bargaining advantages analysed in Chapter 2. In view of the inconclusive theoretical debate and the practical problems involved on opinions the desirability of legal curbs upon unions' activities rest largely on subjective judgements as to whether their power is 'excessive'.

PRICES AND INCOMES POLICY

If reliance on demand management yields politically unacceptable combinations of inflation and unemployment and if legal restriction of union power seems impractical and, to many, undesirable, alternative counter-inflation strategies are required. Governments have relied increasingly upon direct regulation of prices and costs. When inflation originates from administered prices and a struggle over income distribution, an alteration to the procedures of price-setting and collective bargaining is needed to modify the behaviour of firms and trade unions. Full employment can in theory be maintained without inflation by a state assumption of responsibility for price and income levels; Brown (1955) argued that when taxation is unable to remove any excess income above that required to purchase the supply of available goods at existing prices, the additional income generated by the expenditure of this excess must be controlled directly. A number of models of the operation of state price and income controls have been devised[8] and justified on the grounds that, because price and income changes possess social implications, they cannot be the sole responsibility of the parties immediately involved.

A prices and incomes policy formulates general rules to regulate collective bargaining and thus modifies the role of trade unions, whose voluntarist traditions are opposed to state intervention at the point where prices and incomes are set. It initially reduces unions' functions by limiting their ability to increase money wages, but such a limitation will be accepted for longer than a brief crisis only in return for some tangible benefits. Moderation of wage-push could be linked to a strategy of extending labour's influence over a wider range of variables to achieve the ultimate union objective of a more equal society. In this way unions may avoid the impasse of collective bargaining, which exerts only a limited impact upon income distribution, when employers can react to higher wages by raising prices, reducing employment or introducing labour-saving techniques.

Although prices and incomes policies originate as anti-inflationary devices, they inevitably determine income distribution, if only implicitly, through control of the relationship between changes in money wages and the average productivity of labour. This control can only be based on a set of social principles for determining distributive movements. The experience of inflation may cause union leaders to seek the establishment of these principles on the adjustment of wages relative to prices rather than securing the freedom to simply raise money incomes. This aim can only be achieved through institutional changes designed to counter the self-reinforcing character of inequality such as greater union involvement in the decision-making of firms. If trade unions are to moderate their wage-push, the price may prove to be greater union control of manpower management and corporate development programmes.

A striking feature of recent history is the persistent resort to prices and incomes policies despite their limited success.[9] Further government attempts to devise more effective controls are likely, if only because alternative strategies appear to be unpalatable or unworkable. Thus the 1970–4 Conservative Government and the Labour Government which assumed office in 1974 both became more favourably disposed towards prices and incomes policies after experiencing the problems of managing a mixed economy without them. Moreover, around a quarter of all employees now work directly or indirectly for the state, so that a continuous government view of their appropriate pay is inevitable. Therefore, a new type of state intervention, into the determination of price and income levels, appears to be evolving.

THE PROBLEMS OF OPERATING A PRICES AND INCOMES POLICY

A comprehensive prices and incomes policy requires the creation of a new social contract under which different interest groups reach sufficient agreement about the distribution of income and wealth to refrain from attempts to secure immediate advantages at one another's expense. A survey of the environment required to achieve such a consensus is beyond our present scope,[10] but it should be recognised that past incomes policies have not attempted either to shift distribution towards labour or to extend union influence over industrial decisions. Indeed, many have had the opposite objective of improving international competitiveness and reducing inflation at the expense of real wages. This tendency arises from the political consequences of operating a prices and incomes policy in a mixed economy.

Price and income controls can undoubtedly achieve their objectives if applied rigorously. As a consequence of their use in the U.K. war economy, prices rose by only 6 per cent between 1942 and 1945, a remarkable record given existing claims on resources. However, they introduce public policy considerations into all price and income decisions, so that market operations become overtly political, with a consequent narrowing of private initiative in favour of central authority and a move towards the planned economy. The distribution of income and wealth becomes a major issue. Many would find these developments unpalatable.

Prices and incomes policies are easily evaded unless they rest upon a high degree of consensus or an army of enforcement inspectors. Support disintegrates if controls do not apply to all groups but numerous loop-holes exist. Wage regulation is circumvented by upgrading staff, greater fringe benefits, additional increments and overtime working. Price controls can be avoided by changes in product quality, the terms of sales credit and the development of black markets which increase profits per unit of sales without altering productive efficiency. Moreover, tax avoidance, the use of expense accounts, the existence of incremental salary scales and the ability of the rich to buy expertise to circumvent fiscal or legal measures, all maintain the position of the relatively privileged. These sources of inequality must be avoided if consensus is to be maintained under a prices and incomes policy, yet their origins are embedded in the structure of property ownership.

The framework within which governments control pay depends upon a number of variables that they do not determine, such as the level and direction of investment, corporate strategies, and the volume and composition of foreign trade. This leads to a dilemma: failure to plan these variables causes a loss of acceptability for incomes policies and hence a greater likelihood of inflation and unemployment, but state control would transform a mixed economy into a planned one.

A further problem arises when regulating prices. Under present socio-economic conditions price levels tend to become the ultimate determinant of costs and incomes, so that parity of treatment between prices and incomes is crucial to the success of any controls. However, state regulation of prices and profits may discourage the expansion of output. Profits are a different type of income from wages and salaries because they provide the motive force for production. Profits cannot be controlled on the basis of the average for a trade, as their variation is necessary to encourage competition, efficiency and innovation. They fuel the accumulation of capital, so that curbs threaten investment, growth and future standards of living. Gamble and Walton (1976) argued that the concept of a 'fair profit' is irrational, since the only fair profit is the highest that can be obtained. Here lies a further dilemma of prices and incomes policy. It can only achieve acceptability if it treats all interest groups equally, but permanent profit controls will gradually erode the private sector so that the state becomes compelled to provide more investment and employment. Thus effective prices and incomes policies which are satisfactory to trade unions possess far-reaching consequences for the character of the economy.

CONCLUSION

The method of conducting transactions in the labour market and the outcome of these transactions impact so directly upon social welfare and economic performance that all governments evolve a trade-union policy. In the United Kingdom employers and unions developed a voluntary system of collective bargaining, both being reluctant to invoke legal procedures. Consequently the state's role was confined to certain limited tasks, such as facilitating the settlement of disputes, providing machinery to determine wages and conditions in the absence of effective collective bargaining and equipping itself with special powers when a dispute created an emergency. Except for the latter these tasks were designed to support the voluntary system. In the last decade the doctrine of collective *laissez-faire* has come under attack from those wishing governments to pursue positive labour-market policies, while a variety of developments combined to produce a more active government role. The most significant of these were the extended state role as employer, union promotion of specific legislation, growing concern over the United Kingdom's relative economic performance and, linked to this, the greater difficulty of achieving a politically acceptable rate of inflation at a politically acceptable level of unemployment.

Inflation which arises from cost-push forces can be mitigated by techniques of demand management only at the cost of deep recessions involving large-scale unemployment and zero economic growth. The maintenance of a high level of employment between 1940 and 1970 enabled trade unions, whose members were freed from their former insecurity, to raise money wages. Consequently demands arose for legal restriction of union activity and such demands were put into effect in the United Kingdom by the 1971 Industrial Relations Act. It proved ineffective in the face of employers' reluctance to use its provisions and of union opposition, while the theoretical debate concerning the desirability of such measures remains inconclusive and controversial.

The labour-market conditions promoting cost-push inflation seem likely to persist and a prices and incomes policy is the only strategy yet devised which is capable of reconciling price stability and full employment under such conditions. Through their control of the relationship between money wages and productivity such policies inevitably affect income distribution, so that their effective operation in the long term must be based upon a standard of equity acceptable to prevailing public opinion and applying to all types of income. If this standard contains an explicit commitment to greater equality, the role of trade unions changes from increasing money wages as rapidly as possible to influencing a wider range of determinants of their members' living standards, such as decisions upon price levels and corporate development programmes.

Prices and incomes policy offers an escape from the cost-push dilemma, but it involves awkward political choices. The main problems to be solved in making a policy effective are: to achieve a sufficient degree of popular support (if only because the alternatives are feared) so that the inevitable opportunities for evasion are largely rejected, to create institutions that enable union representatives to influence industrial decision-making effectively, and to devise methods of social control over profit incomes that ensure the efficient performance of the functions fulfilled by profits. Solutions are difficult to find, but if these problems are not resolved price stability and full employment is likely to remain an elusive combination. The issue raised in this chapter will occupy a central place in political and economic debate in the coming years, and their resolution would enable a substantial gain in social welfare to be achieved.

8

Conclusion

A SUMMARY OF THE ARGUMENT

We argue that trade unions are not abnormal 'distortions', as often implied by conventional theories, but are a response to fundamental characteristics of labour markets. Employers usually enjoy bargaining advantages when workers are unorganised, so that the formation of unions constitutes an attempt to secure a more equal distribution of power through collective action. Effective unions cannot be realistically regarded as a form of collective monopoly because they do not create a privileged position among otherwise equal parties; rather, they compensate for the bargaining weakness of individual workers by seeking to regulate the terms of sale for labour power.

Trade unions secure negotiating economies of scale, and in order to reap these benefits their organisation tends to become increasingly centralised over time. Successful policies to improve their members' living standards and working conditions have repercussions beyond the immediate bargaining situation since they replace the authority of employers by agreed rules.[1] However, unions cannot remove all the workers' disadvantages, for employers continue to control the revenue from which wages are paid and the ownership of property remains unequally distributed. Conversely some individuals may secure no advantage from union membership. The scope for union action is constrained by the socio-economic environment within which collective bargaining occurs.

We have analysed the opportunities available for trade unions to advance their members' welfare in a capitalist economy. The relationship between relative wages and union strength was assessed in Chapter 3, where it was concluded that some association, of varying intensity in different markets and at different times, could be found. The problems of specification and measurement involved in such research and divergences in the results to date make any assessment of the strength of this association tentative for occupational and industrial differentials. Unions contributed, however, to the narrowing of differentials between individuals, firms and regions.

When union effects upon the general level of money wages are considered, it appears that the maintenance of full employment between 1940 and 1970 changed the character of social relationships in such a way as to provide unions with the opportunity to participate in, and on occasions to inaugurate, a cost-push inflation. This opportunity can be eliminated by budgetary and monetary control of aggregate demand only at the cost of a lengthy period of high unemployment which reduces economic growth, investment and future living standards. The search for policies to reconcile permanent full employment with reasonably stable prices led to a modification of the doctrine of collective *laissez-faire* in favour of more active state intervention in the labour market. To date this intervention has mainly taken the form of restricting union operations, either through such legislation as the 1971 Industrial Relations Act, or through various forms of wage restraint, so that government relations with the unions deteriorated. The framework of a prices and incomes policy that could achieve the ultimate union objective of greater equality was outlined in Chapter 7, though it was emphasised that the adoption of such a policy is dependent upon a change in the power structure.

Although trade unions directly affect only money wages by the application of their bargaining power, one of their objectives is to secure a redistribution of the national product towards labour. It is often claimed that the share of income paid in wages over the present century remained constant, but when salaries are also considered the share going to labour increased. The extent to which this rise is due to the policies and greater coverage of unions is hotly debated, as no generally accepted theory of distribution has been established. Chapter 5 explored ways in which union activity may cause an increase in the proportion of the national income accruing to labour, though the operation of a capitalist economy imposes definite limits upon any such success.

The overall union impact is distorted by concentrating solely upon wages, because non-pecuniary conditions of employment crucially affect workers' standards of living. Therefore, unions seek to influence such items as hours of work, holidays with pay, health and safety provisions, the volume of overtime and arrangements for lay-offs in the event of redundancy. More generally unions seek to modify the discipline imposed upon their members in order to secure the economies of factory production by regulating the employers' control over labour after its hire. The degree to which unions penetrate industrial decision-making depends upon their bargaining power. The relationship between employers and workers varies between managerial autonomy on the one hand and workers' self-management on the other. Collective bargaining is an intermediate situation in which employers retain control of decisions but unions limit their freedom of initiative to some degree. This aspect of union activity must be given due weight in any assessment of its total impact.

THE FUTURE DIRECTION OF TRADE-UNION ANALYSIS

When the production of most firms is small relative to the market in which it is sold, and when workmen do not form trade unions, individuals adjust their demands for, and their supply of, labour in response to prevailing market conditions. Once large firms and organised groups develop, they may not accept prevailing conditions but may instead seek to change them; thus trade unions desire a redistribution of income and wealth, which would alter the operation of labour markets. In these circumstances wages are no longer imposed upon the parties to an exchange, because the successful application of their bargaining power may change them. Consequently the nature of their policy, the sources of their power and the outcome of their actions become appropriate subjects for study.

To take the competitive model for a norm is unrealistic and shows a misunderstanding of its purpose, which is simply to assist in clarifying the relationships between certain variables. The determinants of labour supply are embedded in social relationships so that concentration on the 'economic' influences over the terms of employment omits important sources of disequilibrium. The concept of 'marginal productivity' focuses attention on the fact that workers are employed only when they produce an output which can be sold at a profit, yet the smoothly sloping demand curve derived from it is increasingly unlikely to represent the possibilities open to an employer (Chapter 3 discusses this in more detail).

The distribution of productive resources generates the incentives for supplying capital and labour and so structures the market framework within which supply and demand schedules interact.

Marginal productivity only measures wages (see Robertson, 1931) once the differential power of resource-owners is specified, so that conventional analyses concentrate upon the adjustment of prices and quantities within a situation moulded by forces normally regarded as exogenous to economic models. Incomes are more than a market price since they reflect social values. They are positional and indicate relative status. The wage set by collective negotiations is the end of a socio-political process, in which individual and group aspirations provide the motives and union organisation is a means of achieving them. Defining social classes is a complicated task in which the size of income, the method by which it is acquired and the character of jobs play a prominent part and thus become subjects of bargaining. Marchal (1957) argued that, given the climate of opinion at any time, a social equilibrium exists; if the associated income structure is disturbed, pressures to restore status develop with each group trying to secure relative advantages, as recent U.K. experience of attempts to re-establish eroded differentials indicates. Success in these strategies depends upon bargaining power and the reactions of other groups.

Because large firms and trade unions may alter the social environment within which labour markets operate, theoretical advance requires a revision of conventional notions of data and variables, since it has become more difficult, yet less rewarding, to distinguish actions on, from actions within, a particular market framework. To succeed in bargaining, employers and unions extend beyond negotiating activity by attempting to achieve favourable institutional reforms that change the constraints under which they function, for example union demands for participation in industrial decision-making and for price control during inflationary periods. A complete analysis of labour markets must begin with the social background that determines the position from which capital and labour start to bargain. In such an analysis the nature of the bargaining institutions themselves becomes a variable, so that a wider range of phenomena needs attention.

If each industry is a small, independent part of the economy, it can be analysed in isolation; when this is not the case, we need to consider what is happening elsewhere. Both employer and union expectations are in practice affected by the state of the national economy and the relative performance of other sectors. Indeed, the conclusion of an agreement in one industry may have repercussions upon another through arguments about differentials or the need to retain labour.

The success of a particular union in controlling its members' job environment sometimes depends upon the support of other workers, public opinion and government policy, all of which unions seek to influence. These distinct spheres of operation are more integrated today than formerly; the discussions of the last decade on national economic policy between government, employers and unions brought bargaining and political activity closer together.

Our argument can be illustrated by the operation of the prices–incomes spiral. A trade union with a sizeable membership may find that its wage settlements exert a multiplier effect on other incomes, so destabilising the general money-wage level. Only if the whole union movement applies a co-ordinated policy, can it bargain about the real value of wages rather than their monetary amount and thus mitigate a source of inflationary pressure. Recognition of the interdependence of collective negotiations[2] raises the issues of income distribution and cost-push inflation; it is in this context that recent incomes policies must be assessed. Under such circumstances theories which ignore the significance of the power structure prove an inadequate tool of analysis and an unreliable basis for policy recommendations.

We have attempted to assess the impact of trade unions on certain important aspects of economic life, but our conclusions can only be tentative when faced with the analytical and political problems existing in this confused and controversial area. The most developed part of economic logic is the theory of price determination, but it possesses only a restricted application to labour markets since labour power is not simply a commodity to be traded but is embodied in its owner. Consequently the conditions for the existence of a stable labour-market equilibrium are both economic and social. Its exact position depends upon the balance of supply and demand, the development of new products, technical progress, employer and worker aspirations, prevailing conceptions of fairness and relative bargaining strength. It reflects a given technology and a given power structure. Conventional economics contains a partial explanation of the former and largely neglects the latter. To comprehend fully trade-union organisation and policy they must be related to overall economic development and the structure of the society of which unions are a part. Whether future developments of this type will remain within the confines of the neoclassical theory of pricing is an issue upon which opinions are necessarily subjective. In the interests of maintaining a dialogue with the existing body of knowledge we have used a number of marginalist models, notably in Chapter 3, but our conviction is that present confusions on labour issues will only be clarified by theories in a different intellectual tradition.[3]

Political controversies on the role of trade unions arise because factual assessments are inextricably linked to value judgements of the desirable society and the function of unions within it. Economic reasoning alone is unlikely to resolve such questions. Our hope is that we have been able to spotlight the most significant problems arising from the operation of unions, since these raise many of the crucial policy dilemmas of our time and are likely to continue at the centre of debate in the foreseeable future.

Notes and References

CHAPTER 1

[1] Galbraith (1952) noted the emotionally unfavourable connotations attached by many to the word 'capitalist', but no alternative describes so succinctly those who own the means of production and thus possess major responsibility for private industrial decision-making. We use 'capital' to describe non-human, and 'labour' to describe human, productive resources.

[2] We refer to this general approach as 'neoclassical'.

[3] Perfect competition occurs when an infinite number of buyers confront an infinite number of sellers, each one being so small relative to market size that none can affect price.

[4] The study by Rowe (1929) was a pioneering exception.

CHAPTER 2

[1] Blaug (1962) argued that union development is not fortuitous but is generated by forces inherent in capitalism ('a mature capitalist economy without unions is almost as difficult to imagine as capitalism with a negative rate of interest', p. 263), while the classical economists were also aware of its organic character. For instance, John Stuart Mill (1848) wrote that 'far from being a hindrance to a free market for labour, [trade unions] are the necessary instrumentality of that free market'.

[2] The Contracts of Employment Act of 1963 established minimum periods of notice for employees: at least a week after twenty-six weeks of continuous employment with one employer, at least two weeks after two years of service and not less than four weeks after five years of service.

[3] The operation of labour markets characterised by employers' monopsony power is analysed in Chapter 3 (see also Burkitt, 1975).

[4] A membership function is the appraisal by a union's leadership of the number of workers attached to the union at each wage rate.

[5] The provisions of the Industrial Relations Act increased union difficulties when seeking to extract recognition from recalcitrant employers.

CHAPTER 3

[1] Thus a relative wage gain of 10 per cent implies that unionists receive a wage 10 per cent higher than that of non-unionists doing similar work.

[2] We define the conventional model as 'the hypothesis that prices and quantities behave as though they were in long-run equilibrium under conditions of perfect competition'.

[3] The firm's demand for labour is measured by the marginal revenue productivity of labour, i.e. the net anticipated addition to its money revenue attributable to the employment of one more worker.

[4] Partial monopsony in labour markets is analagous to the more familiar concept of imperfectly competitive product markets.

[5] Hence Marshall's (1920) statement: 'the doctrine that earnings tend to be equal to the net product of a worker has by itself no real meaning, since in order to estimate net product we have to take for granted all the expenses of production of the commodity on which he works other than his own wages'.

[6] See, for instance, the surveys by Kerr (1957a) and Reynolds (1957).

[7] The national degree of unionisation rose from 17.1 per cent in 1911 to 34.3 per cent in 1921.

[8] Industries such as cotton and steel in which skill differentials tended to be maintained were those where skilled workers were recruited by promotion rather than apprenticeship, so that the lower paid were reconciled to the maintenance of differentials by their hope of ultimately enjoying them.

[9] In the United Kingdom the rank correlation for adult males' average weekly earnings over twenty-one major industrial groups between 1959 and 1975 was 0.77.

CHAPTER 4

[1] Friedman (see, for instance, Friedman, 1969 and 1974) is the most famous exponent of monetarism.

[2] For example, Devine (1974) argued that 'the expansion of the money supply is essentially a symptom, rather than a cause, of inflation. It is either the result of the state seeking to make expenditures that socio-political pressures make necessary and that these same pressures prevent from being financed by taxation or by borrowing from the private sector: or it is the result of the state being obliged to accommodate pressures elsewhere in the economy for fear of the socio-political consequences that would follow if it did not'.

[3] Cripps (1977) has provided information on these points.

[4] Including those with such diverse opinions as Balogh (1970) and Haberler (1972).

[5] Thomas (1974) for the United Kingdom, Pierson (1968) for the United States and Vanderkamp (1966) for Canada found that the significance of price changes in the wage-determination equation varied directly with the degree of unionisation.

[6] Cf. our conclusion with that of Devine (1974): 'a chronic inflation is a necessary feature of a social reality in which workers are impelled to struggle to realise their rising aspirations, cannot be prevented from struggling and the system necessarily cannot meet these aspirations. Within this context it is unscientific to attribute "blame" or "responsibility" for inflation to different classes or to the state. Inflation is a product of the capitalist system in its present stage of state monopoly capitalism'.

CHAPTER 5

[1] King and Regan (1976) discussed the various possible methods of subdividing national income. They concluded that it is meaningful to distinguish two income shares, labour and property income, that this distinction bears considerable similarity to the Marxian and neo-Keynesian classification of income by class shares, but much less resemblance to neoclassical concepts of fact or shares, and that methods to allow for changes in the economic significance of the state and of the self-employed exist.

[2] Westergaard and Resler (1975) have comprehensively analysed each of these phenomena.

[3] A high marginal propensity to consume implies that changes in income mainly affect consumption, whereas with a low marginal propensity to consume the main impact of income changes falls upon investment.

[4] Labour income is distributed less equally in a depression due to the effects of unemployment and part-time working, but the reduced opportunity for windfall gains leads to greater equality within the other shares.

[5] The 'long period' is simply that for which reasonably reliable statistics are available; in the United Kingdom this is from 1860 to the present day.

[6] This exposition is based on the assumption that capital and labour are the only factors of production. If land is added to the model, it complicates its operation but does not alter its basic structure.

[7] Trade unions became liable in civil law for their members' actions in carrying out an industrial dispute. Thus almost all union bargaining weapons were inoperative until the Trade Disputes Act 1906 reversed the Taff Vale decision.

[8] The degree of unionisation rose 17.1 per cent in 1911 to 34.3 per cent in 1921.

[9] For instance, by Kerr (1957b) and Simler (1961).

CHAPTER 6

[1] Analysis of the process by which marketable commodities are produced lies outside the scope of conventional economics (which concentrates upon the individual as consumer to the relative neglect of the individual as producer) but has recently been conducted in depth by Braverman (1974) and Friedman (1977).

[2] Wootton (1955) observed that 'with the advent of collective bargaining in place of individual employer–worker negotiations, diplomatic negotiation replaces commercial haggling'.

[3] For example, Mill (1848): 'the form of association which, if mankind continues to improve, must be expected to predominate is not that which can exist between a capitalist as chief and workpeople without a voice in management, but the association of the labourers themselves on terms of equality, collectively owning the capital with which they carry on their operations, and working under managers elected and removable by themselves'.

[4] See, for instance, Cole (1913).

[5] In this situation any conceivable reallocation could only increase one individual's welfare at the cost of reducing the welfare of at least one other.

[6] McGregor (1960) provided a survey of the research on this point.

[7] Bray and Falk (1974) analysed the relationship between self-management and the form of industrial ownership.

CHAPTER 7

[1] In the United States union voluntarism was converted into support for state intervention in labour markets under the impact of New Deal legislation promoting union growth.

[2] Conciliation is a process whereby the two sides are brought together and a third party attempts to secure an acceptable compromise by persuasion. Under arbitration both sides present their case to a third party, who makes an award on the perceived merits of the case. An alternative, the committee of inquiry, ventilates the facts and offers an independent opinion as to a possible solution.

[3] Westergaard and Resler (1975) discussed the crucial legal cases of Broome v. Director of Public Prosecutions and Kavanagh v. Hiscock.

[4] An escalation of strike activity to meet workers' higher aspirations was not peculiar to the United Kingdom in the late 1960s and early 1970s. Comparing the years 1961 to 1963 with 1969 to 1971, annual average working days lost through industrial disputes per 100 employees rose by a factor of 26 in Sweden, 6 in Holland, 2 to 4 in Australia, Belgium, Ireland, New Zealand, the United Kingdom, the United States and West Germany, and by less in Italy.

[5] The intention was that legally enforceable collective bargains would prevent unofficial strikes and a 'cooling-off' period would deter official stoppages.

[6] During confrontations with the N.I.R.C. members' support for their unions remained high and most T.U.C.-affiliated unions refused to register under the Act.

[7] It has been higher than in Scandinavia or West Germany but lower than in Australia, Canada, Italy and the United States; nor, as the figures in note 4 show, has it risen notably quickly in recent times.

[8] Lerner (1944) developed a price-stabilisation model in which relative wage changes are determined by an index of the net attractiveness of different jobs.

[9] Henry and Ormerod (1978) provided a concise history of U.K. incomes policy and a summary of the econometric evidence of its effects.

[10] Burkitt (1975) discussed this issue at length.

CHAPTER 8

[1] Unionisation may also provide benefits for employers; thus organisation helped to create some markets for skilled labour, while many employers prefer to strike a bargain binding on all workers rather than negotiate with individuals or separate groups.

[2] The degree of labour-market interdependence is a function of the geographical proximity, production techniques and organisational links between them.

[3] The recent work of Braverman (1974) on the process of production lends support to this conviction.

Bibliography

A. B. Atkinson (1972) *Unequal Shares: Wealth in Britain* (London: Allen Lane).

G. S. Bain (1966) 'The Growth of White-Collar Unionism in Great Britain', *British Journal of Industrial Relations*.

G. S. Bain and F. Elsheikh (1976) *Union Growth and the Business Cycle* (Oxford: Blackwell).

T. Balogh (1970) *Labour and Inflation*, Fabian Tract No. 403.

P. A. Baran and P. M. Sweezy (1966) *Monopoly Capital* (New York: Monthly Review Press).

M. Blaug (1966) *Economic Theory in Retrospect* (London: Heinemann).

A. Bose (1975) *Marxian and Post-Marxian Political Economy* (Harmondsworth: Penguin Books).

H. Braverman (1974) *Labor and Monopoly Capital* (New York: Monthly Review Press).

J. Bray and N. Falk (1974) *Towards a Worker-Managed Economy*, Fabian Tract No. 430.

S. Brittan (1976) 'The Political Economy of British Union Monopoly', *Three Banks Review*.

A. J. Brown (1955) *The Great Inflation: 1939–1951* (London: Oxford University Press).

B. Burkitt (1975) *Trade Unions and Wages – Implications for Economic Theory* (London: Crosby Lockwood Staples).

B. Burkitt (1977) 'Are Trade Unions Monopolies?', *Industrial Relations Journal*.

B. Burkitt and D. Bowers (1976) 'Wage Inflation and Union Power in the United Kingdom: 1949–1967', *Applied Economics*.

N. W. Chamberlain (1951) *Collective Bargaining* (New York: McGraw-Hill).

H. A. Clegg (1951) *Industrial Democracy and Nationalization* (Oxford: Blackwell).

K. Coates and A. J. Topham (1972) *The New Unionism* (London: Peter Owen).

G. D. H. Cole (1913) *The World of Labour* (London: Bell).

F. Cripps (1977) 'The Money Supply, Wages and Inflation', *Cambridge Journal of Economics*.

P. L. Davies (1975) 'Co-determination: The German Experience', *Modern Law Review*.

P. Devine (1974) 'Inflation and Marxist Theory', *Marxism Today*.

Donovan Commission (1969) *Report of the Royal Commission on Trade Unions and Employers' Associations* (London: H.M.S.O.).

J. T. Dunlop (1944) *Wage Determination under Trade Unions* (London: Macmillan).

W. A. Eltis (1973) *Growth and Distribution* (London: Macmillan).

C. H. Feinstein (1968) 'Changes in the Distribution of the National Income in the United Kingdom since 1860', in *The Distribution of National Income*, ed. J. Marchal and B. Ducros (London: Macmillan).

A. Flanders (1970) *Management and Unions* (London: Faber).

A. Fox (1971) *A Sociology of Work in Industry* (New York: Collier-Macmillan).

A. L. Friedman (1977) *Industry and Labour* (London: Macmillan).

M. Friedman (1969) *The Optimum Quantity of Money* (London: Macmillan).

M. Friedman (1974) *Monetary Correction* (London: Institute of Economic Affairs).

E. Fromm (1965) *The Sane Society* (Premier Books).

J. K. Galbraith (1952) *American Capitalism: The Concept of Countervailing Power* (Boston, Mass.: Houghton Mifflin).

A. Gamble and P. Walton (1976) *Capitalism in Crisis* (London: Macmillan).

A. Glyn and B. Sutcliffe (1972) *British Capitalism, Workers and the Profits Squeeze* (Harmondsworth: Penguin Books).

J. F. B. Goodman (1967) 'Strikes in the United Kingdom', *International Labour Review*.

R. M. Goodwin (1967) 'A Growth Cycle', in *Capitalism and Economic Growth*, ed. C. H. Feinstein (London: Cambridge University Press).

M. R. Gray, J. M. Parkin and M. T. Sumner (1975) *Inflation in the United Kingdom: Causes and Transmission Mechanisms*, University of Manchester Inflation Workshop Paper No. 7518.

G. Haberler (1972) *Inflation and the Unions* (London: Institute of Economic Affairs).

S. G. B. Henry and P. A. Ormerod (1978) 'Incomes Policy and Wage Inflation: Empirical Evidence for the U.K. 1961–77', *National Institute Economic Review*.

J. R. Hicks (1932) *The Theory of Wages* (London: Macmillan).

A. G. Hines (1964) 'Trade Unions and Wage Inflation in the United Kingdom 1893–1961, *Review of Economic Studies*.

A. G. Hines (1969) 'Wage Inflation in the United Kingdom 1948–1962: A Disaggregated Study', *Economic Journal*.

A. G. Hines (1971) 'The Determination of the Rate of Change of Money Wage-Rates and the Effectiveness of Incomes Policy', in *The Current Inflation*, ed. H. G. Johnson and A. R. Nobay (London: Macmillan).

C. C. Holt (1970) 'Job Search, Phillips' Wage Relation and Union Influence: Theory and Evidence', in *Microeconomic Foundations of Employment and Inflation Theory*, ed. E. S. Phelps (New York: Norton).

W. H. Hutt (1973) *The Strike Threat System* (New Rochelle, N.Y.: Arlington House).

A. Jeck (1968) 'The Trends on Income Distribution in West Germany', in *The Distribution of National Income*, ed. J. Marchal and B. Ducros (London: Macmillan).

R. F. Kahn (1977) 'Mr. Eltis and the Keynesians', *Lloyds Bank Review*.

O. Kahn-Freund (1969) 'Industrial Relations and the Law – Retrospect and Prospect', *British Journal of Industrial Relations*.

M. Kalecki (1943) 'Political Aspects of Full Employment', *Political Quarterly*.

C. Kerr (1957a) 'Wage Relationships – The Comparative Impact of Market and Power Forces', in *The Theory of Wage Determination*, ed. J. T. Dunlop (London: Macmillan).

C. Kerr (1957b) 'Labor's Income Share and the Labor Movement', in *New Concepts in Wage Determination*, ed. G. W. Taylor and F. C. Pierson (New York: McGraw-Hill).

C. Kerr and A. Siegel (1954) 'The Inter-Industry Propensity to Strike – An International Comparison', in *Industrial Conflict*, ed.

A. Kornhauser, R. Dubin and A. Ross (New York: McGraw-Hill).

J. M. Keynes (1939) 'Relative Movements of Real Wages and Output', *Economic Journal*.

J. E. King (1972) *Labour Economics* (London: Macmillan).

J. King and P. Regan (1976) *Relative Income Shares* (London: Macmillan).

S. Kuznets (1955) 'Economic Growth and Income Inequality', *American Economic Review*.

D. E. W. Laidler (1975) 'The End of "Demand Management"': How to Reduce Unemployment in the late 1970s', in *Unemployment versus Inflation?*, ed. M. Friedman (London: Institute of Economic Affairs).

A. P. Lerner (1944) *Economics of Control* (London: Macmillan).

H. M. Levinson (1966) *Determining Forces in Collective Wage Bargaining* (New York: Wiley).

H. G. Lewis (1963) *Unionism and Relative Wages in the United States* (Chicago: Chicago University Press).

P. J. Loftus (1969) 'Labour's Share in Manufacturing', *Lloyds Bank Review*.

W. E. J. McCarthy (1966) *The Role of Shop Stewards in British Industrial Relations*, Royal Commission on Trade Unions and Employers' Associations, Research Papers No. 1 (London: H.M.S.O.).

H. McGregor (1960) *The Human Side of Enterprise* (New York: McGraw-Hill).

R. H. MacIver and C. H. Page (1953) *Society* (London: Macmillan).

J. Marchal (1957) 'Wage Theory and Social Groups', in *The Theory of Wage Determination*, ed. J. T. Dunlop (London: Macmillan).

A. Marshall (1920) *Principles of Economics* (London: Macmillan).

J. S. Mill (1848) *Principles of Political Economy* (London: Longmans).

C. Mulvey (1976) 'Collective Agreements and Relative Earnings in U.K. Manufacturing', *Economica*.

C. Mulvey and J. I. Foster (1976) 'Occupational Earnings in the U.K. and the Effects of Collective Agreements', *Manchester School*.

W. D. Nordhaus (1974) 'The Falling Share of Profits', *Brookings Papers on Economic Activity*.

S. Ostry (1968) *The Female Worker in Canada* (Ottawa: Queen's Printers).

E. Owen Smith, *British Industrial Relations*, Loughborough Papers on Recent Developments in Economic Policy and Thought No. 9.

J. H. Pencavel (1974) 'Relative Wages and Trade Unions in the United Kingdom', *Economica*.

E. H. Phelps Brown (1957a) 'The Long-Term Movement of Real Wages', in *The Theory of Wage Determination*, ed. J. T. Dunlop (London: Macmillan).

E. H. Phelps Brown (1957b) Comments on 'An Analysis of Union Models as Illustrated by French Experience' by H. Brochier, in *The Theory of Wage Determination*, ed. J. T. Dunlop (London: Macmillan).

E. H. Phelps Brown (1966) 'Minutes of Evidence 38', in *Report of the Royal Commission on Trade Unions and Employers' Associations* (London: H.M.S.O.).

E. H. Phelps Brown (1975) 'A Non-Monetarist View of the Pay Explosion', *Three Banks Review*.

G. Pierson (1968) 'The Effect of Union Strength on the United States Phillips Curve', *American Economic Review*.

R. Price and G. S. Bain (1976) 'Union Growth Revisited: 1948–1974 in Perspective', *British Journal of Industrial Relations*.

D. L. Purdy and G. Zis (1974) 'Trade Unions and Wage Inflation in the United Kingdom: A Reappraisal', in *Inflation and Labour Markets*, ed. D. E. W. Laidler and D. L. Purdy (Manchester: Manchester University Press).

M. W. Reder (1955) 'The Theory of Occupational Wage Differentials', *American Economic Review*.

A. Rees (1962) *The Economics of Trade Unions* (London: Cambridge University Press).

A. Rees (1963) 'The Effects of Unions on Resource Allocation', *Journal of Laws and Economics*.

G. H. Rehn (1957) 'Unionism and Wage Structure in Sweden', in *The Theory of Wage Determination*, ed. J. T. Dunlop (London: Macmillan).

L. G. Reynolds (1957) 'The Impact of Collective Bargaining on the Wage Structure in the United States', in *The Theory of Wage Determination*, ed. J. T. Dunlop (London: Macmillan).

D. H. Robertson (1931) 'Wage Grumbles', in *Economic Fragments* (London: P. S. King).

J. Robinson (1933) *The Economics of Imperfect Competition* (London: Macmillan).

J. Robinson and J. Eatwell (1973) *An Introduction to Modern Economics* (New York: McGraw-Hill).

G. Routh (1965) *Occupation and Pay in Great Britain* (London: Cambridge University Press).

J. C. F. Rowe (1929) *Wages in Theory and Practice* (London: Macmillan).

J. R. Shackleton (1976) 'Is Workers' Self-Management the Answer?', *National Westminster Bank Quarterly Review*.

A. Shonfield (1969) 'Note of Reservation', in *Report of the Royal Commission on Trade Unions and Employers' Associations* (London: H.M.S.O.).

N. J. Simler (1961) 'Unionism and Labor's Share in Manufacturing Industries', *Review of Economics and Statistics*.

R. Skidelsky (1977) 'The Political Meaning of the Keynesian Revolution', in *The End of the Keynesian Era*, ed. R. Skidelsky (London: Macmillan).

J. Skinner (1972) *Collective Bargaining and Inequality*, Fabian Research Series No. 298.

S. H. Slichter, J. J. Healy and E. R. Livernash (1960) *The Impact of Collective Bargaining on Management* (Washington, D.C.: Brookings Institution).

P. J. M. Stoney and R. L. Thomas (1970) 'A Note on the Dynamic Properties of the Hines Inflation Model', *Review of Economic Studies*.

A. P. Thirlwall (1972) 'Changes in Industrial Composition in the U.K. and the U.S. and Labour's Share of National Income', *Bulletin of the Oxford University Institute of Economics and Statistics*.

R. L. Thomas (1974) 'Wage Inflation in the United Kingdom: A Multi-Market Approach', in *Inflation and Labour Markets*, ed. D. E. W. Laidler and D. L. Purdy (Manchester: Manchester University Press).

J. A. Trevithick and C. Mulvey (1975) *The Economics of Inflation* (London: Martin Robertson).

H. A. Turner (1957) 'Inflation and Wage Differentials in Great Britain', in *The Theory of Wage Determination*, ed. J. T. Dunlop (London: Macmillan).

United Nations (1967) *Incomes in Post-War Europe: Policies, Growth and Distribution* (Geneva: United Nations).

J. Vanderkamp (1966) 'Wage and Price-Level Determination: An

Empirical Model for Canada', *Economica*.

J. Vanek (1970) *The General Theory of Labor-Managed Market Economies* (Ithaca, N.Y.: Cornell University Press).

S. Wabe and D. Leech (1978) 'Relative Earnings in U.K. Manufacturing – A Reconsideration of the Evidence', *Economic Journal*.

J. Westergaard and H. Resler (1975) *Class in a Capitalist Society* (London: Heinemann).

R. K. Wilkinson and B. Burkitt (1973) 'Wage Determination and Trade Unions', *Scottish Journal of Political Economy*.

B. Wootton (1955) *The Social Foundations of Wages Policy* (London: Allen & Unwin).

Index